Voices of Memory 1

The evacuation, liquidation, and liberation of Auschwitz

Publications of the International Center
for Education about Auschwitz and the Holocaust

Voices
of Memory 1

The Evacuation, Liquidation, and Liberation of Auschwitz

Andrzej Strzelecki

Auschwitz-Birkenau State Museum in Oświęcim
Oświęcim 2008

Editors (including the majority of the footnotes, bibliographical notes on prisoners, glossary, and timeline): *Maria Martyniak, Alicja Białecka, Jacek Lachendro, Jacek Lech*

Translation of German documents: *Jacek Lech*

Cover design: *Robert Płaczek*

Corrections: *Beata Kłos*

Photographs and documents:
Archives of the Auschwitz-Birkenau State Museum in Oświęcim

ISBN 978-83-60210-80-2

From the Publisher

The International Center for Education about Auschwitz and the Holocaust at the Auschwitz-Birkenau State Museum in Oświęcim is proud to present the first in a series of books that will appear under the joint title *Voices of Memory*. This series arose as a response to requests, which we have frequently received from participants in the specialist seminars and conferences that we have organized at the Museum over the last ten years, for additional source material. Several thousand people have attended various kinds of courses, postgraduate programs, and conferences. Many of them want to continue learning about the tragic history of Auschwitz, the Nazi German death camp, and, in the case of teachers, to share this knowledge with their students.

Each of these books is devoted to one of the numerous issues in the complicated history of this camp, and contains, in addition to a scholarly article discussing the subject in detail, a selection of source material from the archives of the Auschwitz-Birkenau State Museum in Oświęcim. These include German records created in the various offices of the Nazi state and the departments in the camp, as well as excerpts from accounts submitted after the war by former prisoners. In the more than 60 years of its existence, the Museum has amassed many thousands of accounts and memoirs, as well as a rich collection of photographs. For the historian, this material is a priceless source of information and, in the case of some issues, the only source making it possible to learn the truth about the camp, since the camp authorities deliberately falsified certain events in the official records. This applies to the execution of prisoners in the camp, and matters connected with organizing the mass killing of Jews. In such cases, eyewitness accounts of these events are the only way of learning the truth.

The accounts presented in this volume are the testimony of specific people known to us by name, which is all the more reason to remember that the tragedy of Auschwitz is, at one and the same time, the tragedy of the more than one million victims, and also the tragedy of each individual person.

We hope that the publication of the series *Voices of Memory* will help readers to grasp more fully the uniqueness of the Auschwitz camp, its complicated history, and the contemporary significance of this place for Europe and for the world.

Krystyna Oleksy

Historical Outline

Preparations for the evacuation of the camp

Soviet troops liberated the concentration camp at Majdanek in Lublin in July 1944, capturing several SS men from the camp garrison and seizing the mass extermination apparatus intact. This set the alarm bells ringing for the Konzentrationslager Auschwitz garrison.

From August 1944 until mid–January 1945, approximately 65 thousand prisoners were evacuated. Among them were almost all the Poles, Russians, and Czechs in the camp (some 15 thousand people). They were employed in various industrial plants in the depths of the Third Reich at tasks that included the expansion of armaments plants in the Harz Mountains and in Austria.

In the second half of 1944, the SS authorities devoted a great deal of attention to removing the traces and destroying the evidence of the crimes committed in Auschwitz. They stepped up their existing practice of destroying out-of-date prisoner files and registration forms, and began burning the lists of names of the Jews deported to Auschwitz for immediate extermination.

In September, October, and November 1944, the SS killed some of the Jewish prisoners assigned to the *Sonderkommando* that operated the crematoria and gas chambers, since they were direct eyewitnesses to extermination. A mutiny broke out on October 7, 1944, during one of the attempts to liquidate *Sonderkommando* prisoners, as a result of which more than 450 of them died fighting or were killed. Crematorium IV, damaged during the mutiny, was demolished by the end of 1944. Preparations were made in November and December of that year, on orders from Reichsführer SS Heinrich Himmler, to blow up the three remaining crematoria. Most of the technical installations in the gas chambers and furnace halls of Crematoria II and III were transported into the depths of the Reich after being dismantled. However, Crematorium V and its gas chambers remained in fully operational condition until the second half of January 1945. Movable property consisting of large amounts of construction materials and property plundered from the Jewish victims of mass extermination were hurriedly shipped out.

Shortly after the Red Army began its final Vistula-Oder Offensive in mid-January, the Nazi leadership embarked on the final evacuation and liquidation of Auschwitz. Between January 17 and 21, approximately 56 thousand prisoners were led out of Auschwitz and its sub-camps in columns marching on foot, mostly westwards through Upper and Lower Silesia in general agreement with guidelines issued on December 21, 1944, by the NSDAP *Gauleiter* and *Oberpräsident* of the province of Upper Silesia, Fritz Bracht, who was the local Reich Defense Commissar. About 2,200 prisoners, evacuated from the Eintrachthütte sub-camp in Świętochłowice and the Laurahütte sub-camp in Siemianowice on January 23, were the only ones transported by rail. The main routes for the columns evacuated on foot led to Wodzisław Śląski and Gliwice, where the prisoners boarded trains to continue westward. 3,200 prisoners from the sub-camp in Jaworzno had one of the longest routes, covering 250 kilometers, to Gross-Rosen Concentration Camp in Lower Silesia.

The evacuation columns were supposed to consist exclusively of strong, healthy people capable of completing a march of up to a hundred kilometers. In practice, sick and exhausted prisoners also volunteered for evacuation, since they felt – not without reason – that those left behind would be liquidated. Underage prisoners-Jewish and Polish children – also set out on the march along with the adults.

Along all the routes, SS guards shot not only any prisoners who attempted to escape, but also those who were too physically exhausted to keep up with the others. The corpses of thousands of prisoners who had been shot, or who died of exhaustion or exposure, lined the routes of both marching and rail evacuation. About 3,000 evacuated prisoners died in Upper Silesia alone. It is estimated that a total of not fewer than 9,000 and probably as many as 15,000 Auschwitz prisoners died in the course of the evacuation. Numerous mass graves bear eloquent testimony to the crimes committed against the evacuated prisoners. There are almost 60 such graves in Upper Silesia, and about 50 on Czech and Moravian soil. One of the extant Nazi documents on the "death marches" and "death transports" involving Auschwitz prisoners is a report from the Leitmeritz (Litomierzyce) camp in the Protectorate of Bohemia and Moravia (today, in the Czech Republic), dated March 13, 1945. It notes the arrival the previous day of 58 prisoners evacuated from Hubertshütte, an Auschwitz sub-camp in Łagiewniki. The report states that 144 other prisoners from that camp, almost all of them Jews, "perished" (*verstorben*) en route.

The Attitudes of the Civilian Population During the Evacuation of Auschwitz

The evacuation routes ran through or near villages and towns. The people living there not only observed the dramatic events taking place on the roads, but also aided the prisoners. Poles from Silesia and Czechs from Bohemia and Moravia, for the most part, risked harsh punishments from the authorities to aid the evacuees. To a lesser degree, Germans living in these areas did so as well. Behind the backs of the

SS guards, they gave the prisoners water, bread, and other kinds of food. They helped escapees in various ways, providing them with shelter, food, and clothing.

At some localities in Upper Silesia, the aid of local civilians made it possible for scores of prisoners to escape to freedom. In many cases, civilians sheltered them for several weeks, until Red Army units arrived. When they left the village of Książenice near Rybnik in 1945, 14 escapees from Poland, Austria, the Netherlands, France, and Germany handed an affidavit to local resident Brunon Jurytko. It read: "We the undersigned escapees from the Auschwitz camp attest that Jurytko Bruno, village of Książenice, supported us for eight days at the risk of his own life and the lives of his family, feeding us, giving us shelter and overnight accommodation, and rendering all possible aid. He did all of this at a time when German and SS units were pursuing fugitives throughout the vicinity. In this way, he saved all of our lives, doing so without material benefit, as a decent man"[1].

After the war, Yad Vashem (The Holocaust Martyrs' and Heroes' Remembrance Authority) in Israel awarded the Righteous among the Nations of the World medal to many Upper Silesia residents in recognition of their aid to Jewish prisoners who escaped during the evacuation of Auschwitz.

Removing the Evidence of SS Crimes

While the prisoners were marching away, and afterwards, the Germans made a final effort to remove all traces of the crimes they had committed in the camp. They blew up Crematoria II and III on January 20, 1945. On January 26, they blew up Crematorium V, which was in fully operational condition. On January 23, they burned "Kanada II", the complex of warehouse barracks containing property plundered from the victims of extermination.

The almost 9 thousand prisoners who had been left behind in the Main Camp (Stammlager, Auschwitz I), Birkenau (Auschwitz II), and the Auschwitz sub-camps, were mostly sick and terminally exhausted. Regarded as unfit for the evacuation march, they now found themselves in an uncertain situation. The SS wanted to liquidate all or almost all of them, and only happenstance saved the majority of them from death. Between the departure of the last evacuation column and the arrival of the Red Army, the SS managed to murder approximately 700 Jewish prisoners in the sub-camps of Fürstengrube in Wesoła, Tschechowitz-Vacuum in Czechowice and Blechhammer in Blachownia Śląska.

---

[1] Copy of an affidavit in the Archives of the Auschwitz-Birkenau State Museum in Auschwitz – Mat./ 1623.

In contrast to the chaos that marked the evacuation and liquidation of Nazi labor camps in the final weeks of the Third Reich (when columns of prisoners were sometimes marched aimlessly back and forth), the evacuation of Auschwitz was, for the most part, carried out according to plan by an SS apparatus that was still functioning effectively. As a result of this operation, the Nazi authorities managed to evacuate approximately 100 thousand prisoners and put them to work as slave laborers for the benefit of the German war economy. They also salvaged a large amount of the loot stored in the camp. The Nazi leadership could conceivably, however, have interpreted excessive zeal in carrying out these plans as a sign of defeatism. For this reason, some steps were put off until the very last moment. As a result, the Germans failed to completely destroy the camp, despite the fact the retreating army had long been employing a scorched-earth policy.

Liberation

The prisoners left behind in the camp hoped to regain their freedom. This hope became reality on January 27, 1945. Red Army soldiers entered Oświęcim that day. Soldiers of the 60th Army of the First Ukrainian Front appeared on the grounds of the Monowitz sub-camp, on the eastern side of the city, that morning. They liberated the Auschwitz Main Camp and Birkenau at about 3 p.m., meeting some resistance from withdrawing German units at the Main Camp.

The prisoners welcomed the Soviet soldiers as true liberators; the soldiers, for their part, passed through the camp gates in full awareness of the historical significance of their mission. The paradox is that soldiers who were the formal representatives of Stalinist totalitarianism were bringing freedom to the prisoners of Nazi totalitarianism.

Over 230 Soviet soldiers, including the commander of the 472nd Infantry Regiment, Semen Lvovich Bezprozvanny, died fighting to liberate Monowitz, the Main Camp, Birkenau, and the city of Oświęcim; 66 of them fell during fighting in the camp buffer zone. About 7 thousand prisoners awaited liberation in the Main Camp, Birkenau, and Monowitz. Soviet soldiers also liberated approximately 500 prisoners before or shortly after January 27 at sub-camps in Stara Kuźnia, Blachownia Śląska, Świętochłowice, Wesoła, Libiąż, Jawiszowice, and Jaworzno.

Soviet soldiers discovered the corpses of about 600 prisoners in the Main Camp and Birkenau. The SS had shot some of them during the withdrawal; others had died of exhaustion. These were far from the only traces of crime that the soldiers found.

Prisoners in relatively good physical condition immediately left the camp and started on the journey home.

Medical Assistance and the Return Home
by the Prisoners

Soviet physicians, medics, and orderlies gave the first organized assistance to the liberated Auschwitz prisoners. Two Soviet field hospitals, commanded by physician-majors Veytkov and Milai, soon arrived and began treating sick former prisoners. Polish civilians from Oświęcim and the vicinity, as well as other parts of Poland – most of them members of the Polish Red Cross – made an invaluable contribution by volunteering to help.

A Polish Red Cross Hospital, directed by Dr. Józef Bellert, functioned on the grounds of the liberated camp from the beginning of February until the end of September. More than 4,500 former prisoners, most of them bedridden, received treatment from the Soviet field hospitals. The majority of them were Jews from more than 20 different countries. They included over 200 children, a significant number of whom were the Jewish twins upon whom SS physician Josef Mengele had until recently conducted his criminal experiments[2].

The majority of the former prisoners suffered from starvation diarrhea, usually with complications, of which tuberculosis was the most common. Medical staff recalled that the majority of the prisoners looked like skeletons covered with earth-colored skin. They had abdominal oedema with exudating fistulas. The average weight of the adults was 30 to 35 kg. As late as May 1945, one 20-year-old former prisoner, a Jewish woman, weighed 25 kg.; she was 160 cm. tall. Another, who was 155 cm. tall, weighed 23 kg.

The sick former prisoners were moved into the brick buildings in the Main Camp in February and March. The Soviet field hospital staff and the Polish Red Cross volunteers put an enormous amount of effort into converting these structures for hospital use. They removed hundreds of bedridden patients from their filthy, befouled bunks into clean wards.

Food had to be given in doses, almost like medicine, to accustom the patients to normal eating. In some cases, they received one tablespoon of mashed potatoes three times a day before they were ready to eat several spoonfuls at a time. For many weeks after liberation, nurses found bread under patients' mattresses; they hid it there because they

---

[2] SS-Hauptsturmführer Josef Mengele studied philosophy and medicine before the war, and earned a doctor's degree. In May 1943, he was sent to Auschwitz and assigned to the so-called Gypsy family camp as well as the hospitals and outpatient clinics in Birkenau. He exploited Jewish and Gypsy twins in medical experiments on inherited traits. He also studied people with differently colored irises, cases of dwarfism, and sicknesses resulting from malnutrition (noma or "water cancer"). He took the results of his research with him when he left Auschwitz in January. He went into hiding in South America, where he died in 1979.

could not believe that they would soon receive a new portion. The patients had acquired reflexes associated with constant fear in the camp, and these remained stronger than their sense of reality. For the same reason, many of them refused to go for baths, since they associated the bathhouse with the camp "sauna" where prisoners were selected to die in the gas chambers. Nurses encountered similar reactions when they passed out pills and gave injections. Some prisoners flinched at injections or even refused to take them, because they remembered the injections of phenol used to put exhausted prisoners to death in the camp. Under the care of the doctors and nurses, the patients gradually freed themselves of these irrational reflexes. The influence of camp experience on their minds was, however, irreversible. Unfortunately, some prisoners were so exhausted and so seriously ill that they could not be saved.

In the city of Oświęcim and nearby Brzezinka, local residents spontaneously set up two small hospitals where they cared for well over a hundred former prisoners in 1945. Twenty-three female former prisoners with 24 children, many of them infants, received treatment at the hospital in Brzezinka. The Seraphic Sisters also cared for many patients at their institution in Oświęcim.

The majority of the former prisoners left the Red Army and Polish Red Cross hospitals within three or four months of liberation, and set off homewards. Several of the more serious cases were transferred to hospitals in Krakow. Red Cross missions and delegations from various countries came to the liberated camp to inspect the evidence of the crimes committed there; they took some prisoners home with them. In the spring of 1945, several dozen former prisoners were able to go home by way of Odessa, from where a ship carried them across the Black Sea and the Mediterranean to Marseille. The Soviets moved some other former prisoners, whose homes were in western and southern Europe (probably fewer than 300 people) from Katowice to transit camps (*peresylachnoye lageriya*, comparable to American DP camps[3]) in Byelorussia and the Ukraine in the spring and summer of 1945. They traveled home by train, through Romania and Austria, in the fall. The fate of this group of survivors of Nazi extermination is reflected in Primo Levi's *The Truce* (*The Reawakening*), first published in Italian in 1963[4].

The majority of the children who had been prisoners left Oświęcim in separate groups in February and March 1945, some of them to charitable institutions or children's homes. Their parents managed to find only a few of them. The majority of them, mostly Jewish, spent many years – usually until adulthood – in orphanages, children's homes, and children's villages in Poland, Israel, the USSR, and other countries.

---

[3] Displaced Persons (DP) camps housed people who, for various reasons, were unable to return to their home countries after the war. Most of these camps, set up by the Allied occupation authorities, were in Germany, Austria, and Italy.

[4] Levi, *La Tregua*, Turin: Einaudi, 1963.

Investigating Nazi Crimes

In the first months after the liberation of Auschwitz, special Soviet and Polish commissions there had the task of preserving the evidence of the crimes. The members of the Soviet commission carried out autopsies on 536 corpses found in the camp and stated that the cause of death in 474 cases was exhaustion. They classified as evidence of crimes the items found in the camp storage houses: more than a million men's, women's, and children's garments, more than 43,500 pairs of shoes, and nearly 14,000 rugs. They published their findings in a communiqué "On the German Government's Monstrous Crimes in Auschwitz", published in the newspaper *Krasnaya Zvezda* on May 8, 1945. Two years after the war, the Supreme National Tribunal admitted the protocols of the Polish commission and the original documents that the commission collected as evidence in the trial of former Auschwitz commandant Rudolf Höss[5] and forty former members of the camp garrison.

The liberation of Auschwitz may have ended its existence as the largest Nazi concentration camp and death camp, but it did not close its history. The dimensions and nature of the crime that goes by the name of Auschwitz shocked people around the world and served as a spur for various groups to take various kinds of action in response, and to continue that action determinedly. The effort to come to terms with both the material and the spiritual legacy of Auschwitz still goes on, and the history of "Auschwitz after Auschwitz" is being written before our eyes.

Auschwitz has been acknowledged as a symbol of the Nazi variety of totalitarianism-extreme nationalism and racism that crossed over from the sphere of ideology and political platforms into the sphere of deeds: genocide, the trampling of human dignity, and slave labor. This symbol is seen as a warning against forsaking the fundamental values of humanistic thought.

---

[5] Rudolf Höss was commandant of Auschwitz from May 4, 1940 through November 11, 1943, after which he became head of Central Office DI in the SS-WVHA, from where he was seconded to Auschwitz, becoming SS garrison commander. From May 11 until July 26, 1944, he supervised the mass extermination of the Hungarian Jews.

Selected sources

I. Accounts and memoirs

No. 1
Account by former prisoner Wanda Koprowska on how she left Auschwitz during the preliminary evacuation:

Transport! On October 22, 1944, they released us from the *szelkuchnia* [the room for peeling vegetables]. For several days, we sat in the transport block in *lager* [camp] 'A.' ...At three o'clock at night, they led us out of the block and pushed us into the *Sauna* [camp bathhouse] one more time. There, they checked that all the numbers were present and searched us. They took away the sweaters, warm underwear, and all the things the women had so painstakingly organized. All they gave back was food. But I smuggled the photographs of the children, letters, and some notes once again. Then Perszel[6], Stenia[7], and several *Aufseherin*s [female SS overseers] appeared. They began leading us out one by one. Stenia had another occasion to show off. She bellowed like a wild woman, pushed us, and said she 'hoped the train carrying this gang derailed.' Outside, it was completely dark and pouring down rain. They counted us again at the exit gate, and it took a terribly long time. We were soaked through by the time our row of five reached the gate. The water was running down our backs. Mandel[8], Dreksler[9], Perszel, and Hessler[10] stood at the gate, along with lots of *Posten* [guards] who were going to escort us...

---

[6] SS-Unterscharführer Richard Perschel was at Auschwitz from 1942 to 1945. In 1943, he was a block leader (Blockführer) in the Auschwitz II-Birkenau women's camp, and from 1944 to 1945 the head of the camp labor service (Arbeitsdienstführer) [ed.].

[7] Stefania Starostek was transported to Auschwitz from Krakow on April 27, 1942 and received camp number 6865. She was a block elder (Blockälteste) and senior prisoner (Lagerälteste) of the Auschwitz II-Birkenau women's camp [ed.].

[8] SS-Oberaufseherin Marie Mandel, at Auschwitz 1942–1944, was director (SS-Lagerführerin) of the Auschwitz II-Birkenau women's camp. She was arrested after the war, tried in Krakow for her Auschwitz crimes, convicted, and hanged in 1948.

[9] SS-Aufseherin Margot Drechsler, at Auschwitz 1942–1944, was overseer, report officer (SS-Raportführerin) in the Auschwitz II-Birkenau women's camp, and head of the scribes' pool (Leiterin der Schreibstube) [ed.].

[10] SS-Unterscharführer Franz Hössler, at Auschwitz 1940–1945, started out as a labor detail leader (Kommandoführer) and, from 1940 to 1942, report

Next, they began loading us into the train cars, 85 in each one. Our little group took up a place at the window. It was barred with barbed wire, but we could look out and see where they were taking us. After all, we were traveling into the unknown...

The unknown future terrified us. Stasia, Marysia, and Celinka snuggled up tight against me. Working in the *szelkuchnia* had brought us together and made us firm friends. Now we were all leaving together. Where to?

It was getting more cramped and insufferably close inside the car. Next to the window, we were cold, since we were thoroughly soaked and our rags didn't want to dry. I was standing on one leg because there was no place to put my other foot down. The 85 women took up 3/4 of the car, and the rest was assigned to the SS men.

Thank God! We're moving!

They coupled the locomotive and the train shuddered...

It was the beginning of a horrible night. Imagine 85 women of various nationalities crowded together, lacking sleep, and hungry to boot. The thirst was the worst. We were lucky that the two guards were more humane. During the night, they allowed women to move into the forbidden part... The night went on for centuries, and it was so cold... If only I could have laid my head down for a moment – it was so heavy. The train car became completely quiet. Some women managed to carve out a little space for themselves, and they slept. But the train kept rolling tirelessly on. Where to? Where to? It didn't stop until just before dawn. The car broke into an uproar again. And the darkness was terrifying. You couldn't see your own nose.

We had obviously reached our destination, because we heard excited voices all around and orders being given. The *Post* [guard] looked at his watch. It was four in the morning. We couldn't see anything, but the shouts and calls we heard made us think that they were starting to empty the cars. And then: "*Zu fünf aufrücken*" [get out five at a time]. That was all too familiar, and we no longer had any doubts that we were at our destination. We crowded around the door. At last, the bar scraped and the "gate" of our train car moved aside. Before us were a forest, and barbed wire. They had obviously brought us to a siding, because there was no platform there.

Ravensbrück [concentration camp], in all its glory, greets its future workers...

(1945)

Source: Archiwum Państwowego Muzeum Auschwitz-Birkenau (Archives of the Auschwitz-Birkenau State Museum-APMAB), Recollections Fond, vol. 13, pp. 66–68.

officer (Rapportführer). From 1943 to 1944, he was director (Schutzhaftlagerführer) of the the Auschwitz II-Birkenau women's camp. From 1944 to 1945, he was director of Auschwitz I Concentration Camp [ed.].

No. 2
**Accounts of the removal of signs of the crimes committed
in Auschwitz in the preliminary phase of liquidation.**

A. Załmen Gradowski, former *Sonderkommando* prisoner, wrote in notes
   dug up after the war on the grounds of Crematorium III:
   "Lately, they have started clearing away the traces, and wherever
there were a lot of ashes, they have ordered them to be ground fine,
taken to the Vistula, and released with the current. We have dug up
a lot of graves, but there are still two open graves on the grounds of the
second and third crematoria. Several graves are still full of ash... A vast
amount of ash from hundreds of thousands of Jews, Russians, and
Poles is scattered and plowed into the grounds of the crematoria..."

Source: *Amidst A Nightmare of Crime: Notes of Prisoners of Sonderkommando*, Oświęcim 1976, pp. 131–132 (notes written in the fall of 1944).

B. Henryk Mandelbaum, former *Sonderkommando* prisoner, testified in
   March 1947:
   "...They set about dismantling the crematoria. First, they ordered [us]
to remove the shingles and rafters, and ordered us to take the furnaces
apart... we bored holes in the walls by December 1944. They placed
dynamite charges in these holes. They sent all of us to the camp, and
then they blew it all sky high..."

Source: APMAB, Höss Trial, vol. 26, p. 160.

C. Former *Sonderkommando* prisoner Dov Paisikovic stated in 1964:
   "The SS ordered the dismantling of the crematoria in November
1944. We began disassembling the furnaces. We placed the fire-clay
and bricks in neat piles. At first, we carried out demolition work in
Crematorium I [II][11], and went back to Crematorium II [III] for the night.
Crematorium II [III] was still operating at this time, burning corpses
supplied from the camp. After the disassembly of the furnaces, the
demolition of the chimneys of both crematoria began. For this work, they
sent additional prisoners from the camp, from other *Kommandos* [labor
details]. The metal furnace parts were taken after dismantling to the
railroad platform and loaded onto cars. Supposedly, they were being
shipped to Gross-Rosen [concentration camp]... We did this and similar
jobs until January 18, 1945".

Source: APMAB, Testimonies Fond, vol. 44, p. 96.

---

[11] There were two different ways of numbering the crematoria: I–V (including
the crematorium in the Auschwitz I Main Camp) or I–IV (only the crematoria in Birkenau). Paisikovic follows the second convention; the numbers
in parentheses follow the first convention [ed.].

D. Former prisoner Abraham Steinhardt testified in a deposition in May 1945 on his work in the labor detail assigned to demolish buildings (Abbruchkommando):

"At the end of 1944, in connection with the approach to the camp of Russian units, the dismantling of the crematorium began. In connection with this, I had an occasion to see it from the inside... It was such a solid structure that it was impossible to tear it down with our bare hands alone. We only managed to take the chimneys and roof apart. We prepared the building for demolition by making holes in its walls..."

Source: APMAB, Höss Trial, vol. 16, pp. 33–34 (original in German).

No. 3
Account by former prisoner Rudolf Ehrlich on the liquidation of the Auschwitz sub-camp in Wesoła (Fürstengrube)[12] in January 1945:

The Lagerführer [camp director] came to us after dinner on January 18 and ordered us... to put camp uniforms on over our work clothes because we were leaving in a transport. Chaos then broke out in the camp. The block supervisors told us that we could take whatever we wanted from the camp food and clothing stores. At around 18:00, the Lagerführer told us that he did not know where the transport was going or when it would leave, whether today or in ten days' time or more, and then at 19:00 he ordered us to form up in ranks to march... We formed up in groups... I lined up in the first column, and when the Lagerführer came up I told him that I was sick, that I had sores on my feet, that I didn't have any shoes and was unable to march. He replied that I should go to the hospital block. At 20:00 that day, the groups marched away in I knew not what direction, and only about 250 sick men remained in the camp. All the overseers and SS left the camp, so we were left completely unsupervised...

Twenty SS men came to the camp on the afternoon of January 27, 1945. These SS men ordered everyone capable of standing to gather in one of the wooden barracks. 127 prisoners reported. The rest were supposed to stay in their beds in those same wooden barracks where the hospital was. I was in the group of healthy prisoners on their feet and therefore I had to go with them to the indicated wooden barracks. The commander of the SS men called on the Aryans [non-Jewish prisoners] to step outside. When about 40 stepped outside, he said that was too many and ordered them to go back inside with us. They ordered us all to come close to two windows that were open. Assuming that the SS men were going to open fire on us with their rifles, we hid along the far wall of the barracks where the windows were closed. Then the SS men started shooting at us from outside with their rifles, and threw hand grenades through the open windows. After attacking the barracks for a moment, they looked inside to see whether any of the prisoners there were still alive, and they shot anyone who moved. Then they brought a dozen or more straw mattresses, arranged them at the corners of the barracks, and set them on fire, so that the whole barracks began to burn. During the shooting, I was wounded in the right leg by a hand grenade... At a certain moment, the wooden ceiling of the barracks

---

[12] The Fürstengrube sub-camp opened in Wesoła near Mysłowice in September 1943; it held 1,200 prisoners the following July. They were assigned to labor in the old coal mine (Fürstengrube – Altanlage) and on the construction of the new mine (Fürstengrube – Neuanlage). About 1,000 prisoners were evacuated on January 19, 1945; the SS murdered the majority of the sick prisoners left behind in the sub-camp [ed.].

collapsed and one of the beams fell on me, crushing me completely. I lay there like that for a long time. When I felt the fire approaching me, I tried to get up. One of the SS men happened to look in through the window at that moment, and he shot at me and wounded me in the right arm. I pretended that he had killed me, but I felt that I couldn't stay in that position any longer. As soon as I saw that the SS men had gone around the corner of the barracks, I crawled outside and hid behind a pillar that was part of the skeleton of the barracks. Then I heard one of my friends calling for help, but as soon as I moved there was another shot and it wounded me horribly in the right hand. From where I was, I could see that the SS men were starting off in the direction of a barracks full of people too sick to get out of bed. Some time later, I saw ten patients who had left those barracks and were heading in the direction of the kitchen. As they later told me, they left those barracks on orders from the SS men, and went to the kitchen. They were Aryans. Then I saw the SS men bringing up straw mattresses again, placing them against the wooden hospital barracks with sick people inside, and setting fire to those barracks. Not a single patient got out of those barracks, and they were all burned. Of the group that I was in, only 14 prisoners remained alive, and they were all wounded...

(1945)

Source: APMAB, Höss Trial, vol. 1, pp. 125–127.

No. 4
Former prisoner Józef Tabaczyński's account of the evacuation of the Auschwitz sub-camp in Monowitz[13] in January 1945:

On January 18, 1945, they began leading the prisoners out [of the camp] for the evacuation march. Before departure, they gave out dry provisions-bread and a little margarine... They led the prisoners out of the camp 500 at a time. I left with the last group... SS men walked at the side, guarding the prisoners, who marched in rows of five. The SS men were armed with carbines and automatic rifles...

Past Bieruń, we started passing the bodies of prisoners lying at the side of the road. These were the ones who had died from SS bullets as incapable of marching farther. From time to time, we could hear shots...

Exhausted from the long march, we reached Gliwice...

In Gliwice, all the prisoners were placed on open coal cars, with about 60 people loaded in each one... It was terribly crowded in the cars. None of the prisoners could move or change the position they were in. The train left Gliwice in the evening. Stopping frequently, we traveled very slowly.

It is difficult for me now to describe exactly what started to happen during that train ride. Unprotected form the freezing temperatures, the prisoners grew weak. There were scenes out of Dante. Everyone fought for the space he occupied...

(1964)

Source: APMAB, Testimonies Fond, vol. 44, pp. 60–63.

---

[13] The Monowitz (Buna) sub-camp in Monowice near Oświęcim opened in October 1942 near the site where IG Farbenindustrie was building the Buna chemical plant. The prisoners labored at the construction site. In the reorganization of November 1943, a separate administrative unit, Auschwitz III-Monowitz, with its own commandant on site, was formed from the sub-camps at industrial plants. In 1944, it held 11 thousand prisoners. They were evacuated on foot to Gliwice in January 1945, and transported from there to Buchenwald and Mauthausen concentration camps. Some sick prisoners remained behind at the sub-camp and were liberated there [ed.].

No. 5
From the memoirs of former prisoner Wanda Błachowska-Tarasie-
wicz, a participant in the "death march" from Auschwitz
to Wodzisław Śląski:

Escorted by SS men, burdened down by our backpacks, we marched at
a quick tempo in the direction of Pszczyna. Every few moments, there
was a shot – that was how the SS men took care of those who had
weakened and couldn't go on. The wind and the freezing temperatures
were making things difficult for us. The weaker ones began gradually
emptying their backpacks. They discarded blankets. Underwear, extra
dresses or shoes, in order to lighten the load a little. They called a halt
at two o'clock at night. They gave us a barn and stables for accommodation – they packed us in on top of each other. There was no hay. The
doors were open. We were even colder in there, and, instead of resting,
we only felt more tired. Our shoes were soaked through and our feet
were swimming inside them. We marched on at eight in the morning,
without breakfast... It was well below freezing and we wanted to sing
a little to buck up the weaker and older ones, but unfortunately the SS
men drowned out our singing with gunshots. We came across more and
more corpses in various positions, mostly shot in the head, lying at the
edge of the road. We also left behind a lot of women from our transport...

(July 1945)

Source: APMAB, Recollections Fond, vol. 1, pp. 19–20.

No. 6
From former prisoner Zofia Stępień-Bator's account
of the evacuation of Auschwitz in January 1945:

...A white road, and the large black walls of the forest on both sides...
We could hear the squeaking of the snow and the labored breathing of
the tired prisoners... Gunshots kept ripping the nighttime silence apart
and women were constantly thudding into the ditch for their eternal
repose. Then someone ahead of me fell over. I helped her up. She was
a tiny girl, totally exhausted and as completely alone as I was. Every few
steps, she stumbled. She had a huge pack on her back. "Get rid of that,
it'll be lighter", I urged her. "No. I've got bread in there. If I get rid of it,
I'll starve to death". She was breathing heavily and whimpering like
a baby. I threw her bundle to the ground. She wept out loud. "Don't cry.
I've got bread. I'll walk with you and I'll share it with you. You haven't
got the strength to carry anything". I learned, walking along beside her
and supporting her, that she didn't have anyone at all in the world. She
was a Jewish girl from the vicinity of Radom. Her parents had been
killed, and she didn't have anyone or anywhere to return to. She used
up a good deal of energy in her lamentation. In the end, I forbade her
to talk or moan. I declared that she would come back with me to my
home, and that I wouldn't leave her. I begged her to gather up her
strength, to hold out until dawn, because the sun would come up in the
morning and that would make things easier. She calmed down, and
went on for a while with a regular gait, and then she fell again. I picked
her up. Now I was dragging her along. Nobody helped me. Prisoners
barely able to stay on their feet were passing us. And I... I had lost so
much strength, I was all sweaty from the effort, but I was past the point
where I could have left her. And so we found ourselves at the tail end
of the column. When she fell for the final time, and I no longer had the
strength to lift her up, I called for help, and somebody's hand took hold
of me and pulled me forward. I was very tired, and did not realize that
I was not going to save that girl, and that I myself could die with her.
One of the prisoners, a stranger, oriented herself in the situation, grabbed
me by the arm, and pulled me along with her. A moment later, there was
a shot. It was my poor little ward, whom I had promised not to abandon.
She had stopped suffering... the echo of that shot still rings in my
memory...

(1970)

Source: APMAB, Recollections Fond, vol. 74, p. 167.

No. 7
From an account by Jastrzębie Zdrój resident Maria Śleziona,
a witness to the evacuation of Auschwitz prisoners:

...Together with everyone else who lived there, I observed the tragic march of the prisoners from the window of the building where I still live to this day. The women were forced to go along Pszczyńska Street. On the left side of the street, a woman in very advanced pregnancy dropped out of the column. Leaning against the wall of the transformer [electricity sub-station – trans.], she held her hands over her belly. The column kept going, without stopping. An SS man came up and forced the woman who was in labor over to the roadside on the right side of the street. We ran to the other window, where there was a better view. The prisoner lay on her back in the snow. The SS man shot her in the face with his pistol and a second time in the belly... When the street was empty, we went out to look at the murdered woman. She was a young woman of about 25...

(1978)

Source: APMAB, Other Fonds (IZ) – 27/3.

No. 8
From an account by a resident of the settlement of Branica
near Pszczyna, Teofil Balcarek, a witness to the evacuation
of Auschwitz prisoners in January 1945:

...One night... individual shots from the road next to our house woke us up. This fact disturbed us, but we did not dare to leave the house in the direction of the road. We couldn't see anything out the window... In the morning, at around 7:30 or 8:00, as a so-called "carter", I set out on a horse cart with canisters of milk, mine and my neighbors', in the direction of Kobielice in order to deliver them to a prearranged place near the cross. Not far from my home, I saw the corpse of a man dressed in striped clothing at the side of the road. The body was lying on the bank and there was visible blood. Further on I saw several more similar corpses of men. They had been shot. Some were dressed in striped clothing and others in work clothes. The sight of them terrified me, which is why I did not stop. On my way to Kobielice, I also met a column of men prisoners, dressed in stripes and work clothes, going the opposite way. These were two or three groups with scores of prisoners in each one. They were walking under the escort of armed guards, very slowly, "barely dragging their legs along". ...At the edge of the forest, I was personally a witness to the shooting of one of them by a guard. He was walking at the back of the column. An armed escort suddenly went up to him and shot him with a pistol (not a rifle, but a sidearm). None of the other prisoners looked back. That scene intensified my horror. After delivering the milk, I returned home...

(1986)

Source: APMAB, Testimonies Fond, vol. 115, pp. 204–205.

No. 9
From an account of a resident of Radostowice near Pszczyna,
Franciszka Tendera, on helping one of the prisoners who escaped
during the evacuation of Auschwitz:

On January 24, a very thin young man who was unknown to me, dressed in work clothes, came to my home in Radostowice. Some time later, I learned from my husband, who has been dead for 26 years now, that this was an escapee from the Auschwitz evacuation column. He had already been in contact with my husband before he came to our house. I know that this prisoner escaped in Kobielice or Suszec. I believe that he first received help from the residents of Kobielice or Suszec, since he had already changed his clothes before he came to our house and was not wearing any camp garments. As my husband wished, I took care of him. He stayed with us about a week. We talked with him a great deal. He said that he came from Byelorussia. He tried to convey his experiences in the Auschwitz camp to us. When telling about it, he expressed himself in the following way: "If God existed in this world, there would not be such horrible things as occurred in the camp". That statement moved me greatly, as a believing Catholic. Our guest had frostbitten toes. He suffered greatly from them. I bandaged him and applied goose fat to his toes. On February 9, 1945, units of the Red Army liberated our locality. The next day, our guest went out to the road, and a passing Soviet army cart carried him to Pszczyna, where he reported to the hospital. They amputated his toes there. We visited him. After two weeks, he returned to us. He gave our children cakes and apples then. This time, his visit was short-less than 24 hours. About two years later, we unexpectedly received a parcel through the mail from abroad, in the form of a crate of oranges. There was no return address on the wrapping. We knew, however, that it was our former guest who had mailed it to us. After my husband's death – that is, after 1960-he sent us a letter with heartfelt thanks for saving his life. We wrote back. Soon after, in the next letter, our former guest expressed his great regret that he would never again be able to see my husband...[14]

(1986)

Source: APMAB, Testimonies Fond, vol. 117, pp. 60–62.

---

[14] The escaped prisoner was Elieser Eisenschmidt, until recently a member of the *Sonderkommando* (the labor detail assigned to work in the gas chambers and crematoria). Compare with Eisenschmidt's account (account No. 10). In 1989, the Tender family received the Righteous among the Nations of the World medal from Yad Vashem.

No. 10
**Excerpt from Elizer Eisenschmidt's account of his escape and the
way the Tender family of Radostowice near Pszczyna helped him
(see account No. 9).**

[After escaping from the evacuation transport] I walked towards the
artillery fire, but that was not a good decision. I walked around in
circles all night, unable to get out of the woods. I fell asleep the next
night, because I was completely exhausted. Life stopped mattering to
me. All my strength was gone. If I had to die, however, I wanted to do
it as a free man. I found a good hiding place in some dried rushes near
a pond. I made a mat out of the rushes and lay down on it to sleep...
I woke up freezing cold. I walked and walked until I came to a village –
I did not even notice that I was going back towards Pszczyna. I went up
to a house where a woman was standing in the doorway. I said: "Give
me something to drink!" The woman asked, "What do you want to drink?
Coffee?" She invited me inside. I sat down, and she brought me some
coffee and even a hunk of bread. Then her husband appeared and
wanted to know who I was. I replied dryly, "What does it matter to you
who I am? I'll drink this and be on my way". However, the peasant was
obstinate: "I want to know who you are". Out of fear of being rearrested,
I feigned indifference and said, "Do you really want to know? I escaped
from a transport from Auschwitz". Not far from the home, as it turned
out later, was a street where the prisoners had passed by in the "death
march" – there were still corpses lying everywhere. The husband asked,
"Where do you want to go?" I replied that I didn't know. "Do you know
anyone in these parts?" "No", I answered. "Well then, stay with us". And
so I stayed for around five weeks with that Polish Christian, until the
time when the Red Army liberated the area. Then they took me to the
hospital for treatment...

Source: Gideon Greif, *Płakaliśmy bez łez... Accounts by former members of the
Jewish Sonderkommando at Auschwitz*, Warsaw–Oświęcim, 2001, pp. 211–212.

No. 11
Accounts by participants in and witnesses to the "death march".

A. Former prisoner Nadezhda Svetkova from Byelorussia (camp number 69683):

"Night was falling – the second night of our ghastly journey. We came out of the forest. At its edge, right next to the road, we saw several houses. Outside the door of one of them stood two little Polish girls with two buckets. They dipped water from the buckets with big clay mugs and gave them to us to drink. It was the first sign of human kindness on our journey from Oświęcim. No – it wasn't the two buckets of pure water that was so touching. The touching thing was the empathy of the Polish civilians as expressed in those clay mugs, held out to us by the hands of children".

Source: Nadieżda Cwietkowa, *"900 dni w faszistkich zastienkach"* in: *W faszistkich zastienkach*, Minsk 1958, p. 101.

B. Jewish former prisoner Ilona Strużinska from Czechoslovakia (camp number A-26028):

"The Polish residents of various localities in Upper Silesia ran up to us as we marched through, bringing us milk and bread. The SS men shooed these people away and we marched on, without a moment's pause, without being able to drink anything".

(1972)

Source: APMAB, Testimonies Fond, vol. 80, p. 170.

C. Former prisoner Jan Wygas (camp number 130348):

"I remember that a woman ran up to our column with a jug of water on one of the streets in the city of Gliwice, telling the SS men in German: "Let them drink, they're people, too". She handed the jug of water to one of the prisoners. The SS men shouted at her to get out of the way. When she turned away, he shot her in the back of the head. The woman dropped to the ground. I observed that scene".

(1978)

Source: APMAB, Testimonies Fond, vol. 89, p. 138.

No. 12
Examples of written expressions of gratitude to residents
of Upper Silesia, from evacuation march escapees they helped.

A. Letter sent in October 1946 from Friedel Gilsbach-Strauss in
   Amsterdam to Władysław Wuzik and his family in Brzeźce near
   Pszczyna. The most relevant passage reads:
   *"Ich werde Sie nie vergessen so lange ich lebe, denn Ihnen kann ich
   mein Leben verdanken: wenn Sie doch nicht so gut zu mir gewesen wären,
   hätte ich meine Heimat nicht mehr zurückgesehen".*
   "As long as I live, I'll never forget you, because I owe you my life. If
   you hadn't been so good to me, I'd never have seen my homeland again".

Source: APMAB, Mat./1771, photocopy.

B. Letter from Helena Berman to Maria and Franciszek Parzych of
   Jastrzębie Zdrój, January 18, 1946. It contains the following recollec-
   tion and expression of gratitude:
   "I'll never forget the warm reception I got from the woman of the
   house, Franciszka Parzych, and her children. I was sick, mistreated,
   and terrified. Everything in that home was at my service. I lay sick for
   several days, looked after by those magnanimous people and surrounded
   with loving kindness. Mrs. Parzych carried the best things she had, and
   warm clothing, into my clean, snug, well-heated room. This was encour-
   agement to survive. After all, death hung over us in the form of the
   Gestapo, who were snooping around the village looking for fugitives –
   they shot them on the spot, along with the families who took them in...
   I could write endlessly about those moments full of sacrifices and
   fear for us [former prisoners] and for the fate of my saviors, but I must
   keep it short: glory and the blessings of God on our saviors, those great
   Polish hearts, those fervent Polish patriots"[15].

Source: Józef Musioł, Było to w styczniu, *Poglądy*, 221 (1972), p. 6.

---

[15] In 1984, the Parzychs were awarded the Righteous among the Nations of
the World medal.

No. 13
Account by former prisoner Dr. Irena Konieczna, a doctor in the camp hospital, on the last days of Auschwitz and liberation:

The final evacuation on foot of women from Birkenau began on January 18, 1945. They ordered the prisoners to prepare immediately. The SS men were going around trying to talk women into joining the transport. They said that the whole camp was mined and that they were going to blow it up after they left. Many women asked me: should they go with the transport or stay there? I told them that I was staying, because, if I was going to die, I wanted to die on Polish soil, but that they had to make up their own minds. I remember how the SS men from the infirmary were urging me at the last moment to go with them in the transport. In the final minutes before the column started out, they were looking for me in the blocks. I avoided evacuation by lying down alongside a sick prisoner on the top tier of one of the camp bunks. After the departure of the last evacuation transport, there were about 2,000 patients left in the women's camp hospital, and a mere handful of more-or-less healthy prisoners to care for them. There were no more SS guard posts to be seen, only individual SS men who came into the grounds of the camp. I also heard that groups of SS men entered the camp sporadically and shot many Jewish women.

I would refer to the period before the arrival of the first lines of the Soviet troops as an "interregnum". Total anarchy reigned in the camp. No one obeyed anyone, or showed any respect to the previous prisoner functionaries. No one carried corpses out of the block and no one cleaned up the filth. The prisoners required treatment and food, but there was a lack of willing hands to look after them. Some prisoners managed to bring some food products back from the SS warehouses, and tried to prepare hot meals. Together with several fellow prisoners, including Dr. Sara Marinette, I "bent over backwards" to help the greatest possible number of bedridden patients, in terms of both medical care and food. We tried to keep up the spirits of all our fellow prisoners, so that they would not give up but rather hold out until the moment when they returned to their families. Someone told me that men prisoners had carried a certain amount of food, or rather delivered it on carts, to Birkenau from the storehouses in the Main Camp. I remember that there were personal confrontations between some of the women during the days of the "interregnum". As far as I know, some prisoners exchanged sharp words or even blows. I even talked one of my fellow prisoners, who was in danger, into leaving the camp immediately. I know that a fair number of prisoners left the camp during the "interregnum" period and set off for home on foot.

Several Soviet soldiers-scouts with their rifles ready to fire-entered the grounds of the women's camp hospital on January 27, 1945. The prisoners rushed joyously towards them. Some time later, a horse-drawn military column drove up in front of the blocks. When the Soviet soldiers realized what our situation was like, they supplied us with food of the highest quality (excellent army bread baked in pans, melba toast, and natural fats). A day or two later, several beautifully built Soviet officers, dressed in long, clean white sheepskin coats, appeared and carried out a precise reconnaissance of our needs...

(1974)

Source: APMAB, Testimonies Fond, vol. 113, pp. 130–132.

No. 14
Statement by Alexander Vorontsov of Moscow, camera operator in the Soviet military film crew that recorded the liberation of Auschwitz:

A ghastly sight arose before our eyes: a vast number of barracks (in Birkenau)... People lay in bunks inside many of them. They were skeletons clad in skin, with vacant gazes. Of course we spoke with them. However, these were brief conversations, because these people who remained alive were totally devoid of strength, and it was hard for them to say much about their time in the camp. They were suffering from starvation, and they were exhausted and sick. That is why our interviews, such as they were, had to be very brief. We wrote down the things they told us.

When we talked with these people and explained to them who we were and why we had come here, they trusted us a bit more. The women wept, and – this cannot be concealed – the men wept as well.

You could say that there were pyramids on the grounds of the camp. Some were made up of accumulated clothing, others of pots, and others still of human jaws.

I believe that not even the commanders of our army had any idea of the dimensions of the crime committed in this largest of camps. The memory has stayed with me my whole life long. All of this was the most moving and most terrible thing that I saw and filmed during the war.

Time has no sway over these recollections. It has not squeezed all the horrible things I saw and filmed out of my mind...

Source: Scenario of the documentary film Die Befreiung von Auschwitz, by Irmgard von zur Mühlen (Chronos-Film GmbH, West Germany), commissioned in 1986 by the Holocaust Memorial Council of the USA. APMAB, Scenario Fond, vol. 53, pp. 23–26, 29, 40.

No. 15
The liberated camp as seen by Dr. Tadeusz Chowaniec, an Oświęcim resident:

It was Monday, [29] January, 1945. A gloomy, overcast, chilly early morning. The first moments of relaxation, freedom, and understandable chaos... In Stare Stawy, not far from Oświęcim, the corpses of Wehrmacht soldiers, still not removed, lay side by side near some village farm buildings. Right next to them lay a Soviet soldier killed on Saturday evening. Some sort of violent internal impulse, or perhaps only curiosity, impels me in the direction of the gates of the former concentration camp... Two Soviet wagons loaded with prisoners' corpses passed us just inside the gate. The corpses resembled medieval illustrations of death... I simply had to see Block No. 11, and its interior. After all, my father was imprisoned there two years earlier. He spent seven months in that building. He wrote letters and received parcels from us. Today, he is in the concentration camp in Buchenwald. Is he alive? What does he look like? Does he look like those we see here?... The block stands wide open. The corridor, despite the prevalent cold, is filled with the sweetish smell of decaying corpses. It is stifling. I look at the other people who are here. Some faces are horrified, others enraged or emotional...

Yet there were also living people... The first encounter with these living specters, with nearly transparent faces and cloudy, indifferent eyes, made a depressing impression. These figures that barely, sluggishly stirred on the bunks had abscessed thighs and toothless jaws. They spoke in whispers, with strangely hoarse voices. The folds of old age furrowed the skin of people in their twenties. The white smocks of Soviet physicians, men and women, moved among these patients. The nurses-despite the difficult conditions-managed to smile. Can their treatment pass the examination? Is it possible that life will be restored to these near-skeletons?...

We leave the camp in Auschwitz and head cross-country towards Birkenau, towards the pyres that may still be smoldering, that still smoked not long ago... With their doors broken down and ajar, the barracks are terrifying. Around us are masses of pots, bowls, and old buckets scattered on the snow. In one of the brick barracks, we saw women prisoners lying in bunks, several of them to a single tier... They move with difficulty. Every movement seems deliberately economical. Looking at their indifferent eyes, almost cold, with no spark of joy, we feel ashamed of ourselves...

Source: Tadeusz Chowaniec, Epilog, *Zeszyty Oświęcimskie*, 7 (1963), pp. 145–154.

No. 16
From an account by former prisoner Zofia Lutomska-Kucharska
(camp number 49999) of her work in treating sick former prisoners:

On the second or third day after liberation, a Soviet field hospital arrived in the camp. The Soviet physicians applied without delay for con-
signments of easily digestible foodstuffs (potatoes and dietetic gruel) for
the f[ormer] prisoners, and introduced rational meals. The sick f[ormer]
prisoners began receiving medication, including high-quality medicines
of English and American manufacture.

The intermediary between the Soviet physicians and the f[ormer]
prisoner physicians and nurses was a f[ormer] Russian prisoner, Dr.
Arkady Mostovoy, a specialist in venereal diseases. Dr. A. Mostovoy held
this post for a long time.

For a certain period of time after liberation, I continued to work as
a nurse in the 13th block in the grounds of sector BIIe[16]. Since Dr. Irena
Białówna was evacuated into the depths of Germany in January 1945,
Dr. Alicja Piotrowska held the function of block physician in the 13th
block. After January 27, aside from myself and Dr. Alicja Piotrowska,
f[ormer] prisoner physician Krajnik from Hungary and f[ormer] prisoner
[Izabela] London, Kazimiera Królikowska, and Zofia Klimkiewicz cared for
the prisoners in the 13th block.

I cannot remember exactly when they transferred us from Brzezinka
to the f[ormer] Main Camp, and exactly when and where, that is, in
Brzezinka or in the f[ormer] Main Camp I first came across members of
the PRC [Polish Red Cross] team that came to help us. We greeted the
PRC crew with great joy. At the moment of the arrival of that crew, the
number of physician-nursing personnel in each block was increased,
and in connection with this, the general conditions for working to care
for the patients improved. It then became possible to think about divid-
ing the separate functions and rationalizing the organization of the
work. The PRC also sent a great deal of medicine to the camp for the
prisoners. Gradually, more and more patients regained their health.

Among the members of the PRC who came to help us, I remember the
name, or the first names, of only Dr. Józef Bellert and the nurses Irena
and Jasia.

In the f[ormer] Main Camp, I also worked in the block designated with
the number 13. All the sick f[ormer] women prisoners, and the physicians and nurses from the 13th block in Brzezinka were transferred to
that block. In the former Main Camp (in the 13th block), the PRC nurses

---

[16] The Birkenau camp was made up of three segments designated BI, BII, and
BIII. The first two were divided into sectors. The so-called Gypsy family
camp was located in sector BIIe until August 1944. In November 1944, sick
women and children prisoners from BIIa were relocated there. Some of them
survived until liberation [ed.].

Irena and Jasia, already mentioned, cooperated with me. I best remember the character of Irena. She was very hard working and noble.

For a long time, in addition to Dr. Arkady Mostovoy, Dr. Krajnik, and Dr. Alicja Piotrowska, a range of other former prisoner physicians, including Dr. Otto Wolken, treated the patients. I also remember that Dr. [Alfred] Galewski stayed in Oświęcim for several months after liberation. However, he had a serious lung disease, in connection with which he could not help the f[ormer] prisoners as a physician.

In my opinion, Dr. Alicja Piotrowska (Przeworska) deserves special mention among the former prisoner physicians. She was a wonderful woman. I have not the words to acknowledge her. Both before and after liberation, she worked selflessly to care for patients regardless of their nationality or origins. She often worked day and night, almost without a break, to do her duty. She was a true friend and protectress to all her patients and fellow physicians.

Among the personnel from the Soviet field hospital who cared for the sick former prisoners, I remember the names Dr. Major Zhilinska and Dr. Major Polakova.

The clergy from Oświęcim, and especially the Salesian priests, also came forward to help the sick former prisoners. The priests brought us foodstuffs, including honey. The honey was given only to children. Each week, they said mass for the patients. The priests heard confessions and gave communion to the patients. I am in possession of a postcard with the image of Saint Anthony and the Infant Jesus, which was given to me by Father Stanisław Rokita, director of the Salesian community. On the back of the card he wrote: "To Zosia Lutomska, martyr of the Auschwitz camp, the blessing of the Heart of Jesus with the intercession of St. Anthony. Father Stanisław Rokita – first chaplain of the Auschwitz camp. Oświęcim. Feb. 2, 1945".

The former child prisoners were transferred from Oświęcim to Krakow. PRC nurses took them there and placed them in various care centers. Together with the PRC nurses, I took a group of children to Krakow, but I do not remember exactly to which center. On the grounds of the former camp in Oświęcim there was a lack of the full conditions for the treatment of children. They found much better care outside the camp...

On May 31, 1945, I left the PRC Camp Hospital in Oświęcim and traveled to Warsaw. In Warsaw, I found my home in ruins, and therefore went to stay with relatives in Grójec, where I found my mother. I possess two documents attesting to my work in the hospital for liberated prisoners of Auschwitz Concentration Camp...

Source: APMAB, Testimonies Fond, vol. 74, pp. 233–238.

No. 17
From an account by Polish Red Cross volunteer Zdzisław Bosek
of Brzeszcze about his participation in the effort to aid liberated
Auschwitz prisoners:

Several days after liberation, that is, on February 2–3, 1945, I voluntar-
ily went, along with several friends, to the grounds of the former Main
Camp in Oświęcim in order to join the effort to help the liberated prisoners. We entered the camp by sleigh, through the gate near the villa
occupied until recently by the camp commandant. Prisoners' corpses,
frozen to the ground, lay scattered all over the road from the gate to the
site of the crematorium, and this prevented us from going by sleigh into
the depths of the camp. There were dozens of corpses, but I cannot
remember exactly how many. When we removed them from the road
soon afterwards, we had to use shovels to separate them from the ground.
Immediately after entering the grounds of the camp, we reported to the
commander of the Soviet military unit stationed there. We were immediately accepted for service in aid to sick ex-prisoners. We were even
given Soviet uniforms. Aside from Soviet soldiers and ex-prisoners, we
also found other Poles in the former Main Camp who had come volun-
tarily, some of them from Krakow, to help the ex-prisoners. A short time
later, a PRC Camp Hospital was set up in addition to the Soviet field
hospitals that were already operating. We worked in the hospitals as
orderlies for several months.

In the first days we spent working in the former Main Camp in
Oświęcim, we joined other volunteer orderlies in creating hospital rooms
in the buildings located near the former crematorium. We brought sick
ex-prisoners there from other buildings. Afterwards, we joined the effort
to bring sick ex-prisoners from Brzezinka to Oświęcim. We brought the
sickest ones out of the barracks on carts and sleighs, which had been
brought in large numbers from the vicinity. Within a certain time, the
conditions for treating the patients resembled those in normal hospitals. Specialist departments were set up: surgical, tuberculosis, and
a department for patients with starvation diarrhea (*Durchfall*); an am-
bulatory clinic was set up. Volunteer physicians, nurses, and orderlies
were assigned to regular shifts in the various departments. About ten
volunteer orderlies from Brzeszcze, including my school friend Kazimierz
Baraniak and my father's brother, Mieczysław Bosek, worked with me in
Oświęcim.

I want to indicate that the majority of the patients were prisoners
who, when we started treating them, were in a state of extreme... ne-
glect. They lay on the tiers of their bunks in camp clothing, covered with
dirty rags, and generally without mattresses or even straw. Many of
them were too weak to get out of their bunks. As a result of this, the
bedridden patients suffering from starvation diarrhea were lying in excrement. Some of them were badly infested with lice. We transferred

these patients to the rooms we had cleaned up in the meantime and placed them in regular beds that we had made by cutting up the multi-tiered camp bunks.

The Polish physicians, nurses, and orderlies worked in the various hospital buildings alongside the members of the Soviet medical and nursing staff. Only one building was reserved exclusively for Soviet soldiers. Among the physicians, I remember the Polish head physician (Józef) Bellert, and a tall Russian in glasses. In any case, in the picture that was shown to me where there are three doctors and the chief nurse of the PRC, I recognize the Russian and Polish physicians whom I knew personally, and additionally the Polish physician Zdzisław Makomaski. I had contact most frequently with Dr. Bellert...

As I have already indicated, we orderlies were on duty in particular hospital departments, doing such things as bringing meals to the patients and leading or carrying them to the baths and X-ray. We helped the nurses feed the most seriously ill, we tidied up the patients' bedding, and we gave them medicine both orally and by injection, and also by intravenous... We were also there when the doctors made their rounds.

Because of the illnesses they had contracted while they were in the camp, many ex-prisoners were so physically exhausted that there was no saving them. Therefore, despite our efforts to furnish the sick ex-prisoners with the best possible conditions for treatment, the death rate among them remained quite high.

On the day when we arrived at the grounds of the liberated camp (February 2–3), we visited Block No. 11, the so-called "Death Block". We found the corpses of many prisoners in this block – the victims of the last days of SS operations in Auschwitz. We saw some of them in the first, rather large room to the left of the entrance to the block. The corpses of women predominated there, including pregnant women... Several days later, we carried to Block No. 11 the corpses of the prisoners that we had gathered from the road leading from the gate, past the camp commandant's villa, to the crematorium. Block No. 11 was used as the hospital morgue...

I saw a very large number of prisoners' corpses – the victims of the evacuation of the camp – in Brzezinka (Birkenau). Among other things, I saw corpses in an open mass grave there. It was located at the end of the camp railroad platform... In two places in Birkenau, beside the crematoria at the end of the railroad platform, we also found partially-burned corpses on crematory pyres. For a certain time not long before February 28, 1945 – that is, before the ceremonial funeral for the victims of the Oświęcim camp – we gathered corpses from the Brzezinka grounds. First, we carried these corpses to one of the wooden barracks (in the vicinity of the crematoria), where autopsies were carried out on tables placed there for the purpose. A special Commission did this work. Afterwards, we placed the corpses in wooden chests-coffins – that we made from boards in the meantime. We placed 4–5 corpses in each chest-coffin. Next, we carried them on carts to the grounds of the Main Camp, to Block No. 11, used as the hospital morgue... All of this was in preparation for the ceremonial funeral.

On February 28, 1945, I took part in the ceremonial funeral of the victims of the Auschwitz camp. We carried all the prisoners' corpses, which we had found and gathered inside and in front of Block No. 11, to graves near the site of the Main Camp that had been prepared ahead of time. Many corpses were also brought from Brzezinka at this time. After the corpses had been placed in the graves, various personages delivered eulogies, including one of the ex-prisoners and a Soviet officer, probably the commandant of the Soviet field hospital. The orchestra from the Brzeszcze coal mine was there. Soviet cinematic reporters filmed the funeral and took many pictures...

After February 28, 1945, in the little cemetery near the f[ormer] Main Camp, we orderlies, together with Soviet orderlies, buried the corpses of the ex-prisoners who had died in the Soviet field hospitals and the PRC hospital...

Almost every day, people came to the grounds of the liberated camp who had applied to the Soviet authorities or to the administration of the PRC hospital with requests for aid in finding their relatives or acquaintances among the former prisoners, or with requests for information about the fate of missing relatives.

The ex-prisoners who had been cured, or who had convalesced to the point where they were capable of traveling, left Oświęcim in specially organized transports. They were moved in motor vehicles, under the care of volunteers from the hospital staff, either to Katowice or to Krakow. A group of children was taken to Warsaw...

In many cases, the ex-prisoners leaving Oświęcim expressed very sincere thanks to the members of the hospital staff for their help. They gave the Polish volunteers various mementos and left them their addresses, inviting them to visit them or their families abroad...These were very emotional farewells...

(1974)

Source: APMAB, Testimonies Fond, vol. 82, pp. 219–227.

No. 18
From the memoirs of Ursuline sister Tacjana (Helena)
Pożarowszczyk, who joined her Mother Superior Aniela Skrzyńska
and several other nuns in working to aid liberated prisoners:

We set out full of joy and enthusiasm to help those most miserable ones,
who suffered the most for the Fatherland at the hands of the Germen
henchman. We set out from Krakow by bus at 10 o'clock on the morning
of February 14, 1945. Together with us were eight nurses from the
Polish Red Cross, led by Dr. [Jan] Grabczyński, and also Father Kowalski...
After a two–hour trip, we saw Oświęcim – a city of prison barracks. After
dropping off our luggage, we settled temporarily into a large room. The
next day, they assigned two nice rooms for us... The Soviet authorities
transported all the prisoners from Brzezinka to the Oświęcim *lager* (to
the former Main Camp), so that Major Milay was in charge of two thousand prisoners. Many of them were gravely ill. Between ten and twenty
people died each day. The highest percentage were Jews. There were
also many from Warsaw, from the period of the Uprising. The patients
were very grateful for favor. They cried for joy when they saw us the first
time. We heard the voices of the Jewish women constantly: "...Sister...
come here, please", and each of them wanted to tell about her experience, hurt, and suffering. There was no time for that, because at the
beginning there was a lot of work to do on the wards, and only on night
duty did we listen to their stories. Night duty with the patients was not
very pleasant. One nurse had the whole ward, consisting of five large
rooms, and the lights very often went out at night... The Oświęcim camp
is currently under Russian administration. At the head of the director-
ate were two majors. One part of the camp belonged to Major Vitkov
[Veytkov], and the other part to Major Milay. We worked for Major Milay,
for whom the prisoners had great respect, while the seven Seraphic
sisters worked for Major Vitkov. After two days, we went to work. The
Rev. Mother Superior had to split us up: Sisters Felina, Agnieszka, and
two Sisters of the Order of the Most S[acred] Spirit of Christ went to the
kitchens, and the rest to the patients on the wards. The Rev. Mother
Superior had the most work; her greatest concern was to meet the
needs of those poor ones hallowed by suffering and still desirous of some
spiritual consolation before they passed away. Those who could walk
even a bit had the joy of being [able to hear] Sunday mass. Mother
Superior spent all day arranging this and prepared people who had not
been to confession for years to do so. Thus there were French people,
Germans... Poles, etc. There were a lot of people at the first mass. The
vicar from the Oświęcim church said mass and gave a very lively sermon. There was loud weeping, and he told them that they are our relics
and our pride, and he urged them to leave vengeance for their great
wrongs to God, to let God take vengeance for their sake. They were
immeasurably grateful to Rev. Mother Superior for her efforts to give

them this spiritual comfort. There was mass, with a sermon, at 4 o'clock each Sunday afternoon. They started taking the patients away by truck and cart after two weeks; they took them to Krakow and Katowice. There was less work to do each day. Rev. Mother Superior began thinking about our departure... She informed the Red Cross, Doctor [Józef] Bellert, and Major Milay of our departure. Major Milay wrote up an official document thanking us for our work. The patients said goodbye to us with great regrets... The other nurses, who had become very close to us during this month, said an emotional farewell to Rev. Mother Superior. On March 14, 1945, at 8:00 in the morning, we returned to Krakow under the care of Dr. Bellert...

(April 1945)

Source: Original in the archives of the Ursuline Sisters' convent in Krakow, photocopy in APMAB, Recollections Fond, vol. 186, pp. 54–62.

No. 19
From an account by Polish Red Cross volunteer Maria Rogoż,
registered nurse, who lived in Krakow after the war:

I had been staying in Krakow since 1939 as a refugee from Volhynia, living at the Home for Expelled Persons and Refugees run by a social welfare organization, probably the M[ain] W[elfare] C[ouncil][17]. I was active in the Home Army at the time and worked with other people to prepare parcels for Polish soldiers held captive in the depths of Germany. After liberation in 1945, my comrades in the organization suggested that I go to work on the grounds of Auschwitz Concentration Camp, in the hospital for former prisoners. Although they stressed that this meant caring for extremely exhausted persons in camp conditions, I agreed without hesitation. I reported on February 24 to the appointed place, where a dozen or so people were waiting to travel to Oświęcim. Among them were some who already worked in the hospital there, and were returning from short visits to their families. We traveled to Oświęcim in a truck, probably a Soviet army truck.

It was a long ride in difficult conditions. The temperature was below freezing. The truck stopped frequently, since there were bottlenecks of Soviet military transports on the road, and, coming in the opposite direction, crowds of people returning from the camps in the West. The bridges were out, and this made it necessary to take a roundabout route. On top of that, military patrols stopped the truck in many places. We reached the place late in the evening. They sent us to lodgings in one of the buildings on the grounds of the former Main Camp. I slept in the second tier of a camp bunk. In the morning, along with other people brought to work in Oświęcim on February 24, I was introduced to the head physician of the PRC hospital in Oświęcim, Dr. Józef Bellert. That was the first time I had seen him. We went to work in the hospital without delay. I did not personally possess adequate preparation for that work, since all I had done before the war was to serve as a hygienist at a Scouts' unit run by Olga Małkowska in Sromowce Wyżne (Dworek Cisowy). Nevertheless, they signed me up immediately as a nurse. I also received instructions as to my most important duties. I took these instructions very much to heart. For a month, my place of work was Block No. 12 and Block No. 13. I was added to the Soviet nursing personnel there...

The sight of the rooms full of patients made a shocking impression on me... when I went in there for the first time. There were about two

---

[17] The Main Welfare Council (*Rada Główna Opiekuńcza – RGO*) – Polish charitable organization that operated legally in the General Government during the Nazi occupation. It ran charitable institutions, soup kitchens, and shelters, as well as aiding expellees and sending parcels to prisoners and POWs [ed.].

hundred ex-prisoners in.the building... There were women on the ground floor and men upstairs... They lay in multi-tiered camp bunks, covered in blankets of a very good sort that came from the so-called "Kanada", the camp storehouses. These blankets, like the straw mattresses, were very dirty with excrement. A thick, unpleasant odor prevailed in the rooms. Iron stoves helped heat the rooms. I immediately went on duty in a room with eighty women in it.

Eleven women died during the first night shift in that room. I had to remove the corpses from the bunks myself and carry them to the corridor. Early in the morning, orderlies carried these corpses out of the block. All night, from various corners of the room, I heard calls: "*Schwester! Schieber!* Sister! Bedpan!" The patients were suffering from *Durchfall*, or starvation diarrhea. So I spent all my time giving them the bedpan. There was no one to help me.

There were many difficulties associated with caring for the ex-prisoners. Above all, the patients had to become accustomed to food. In the difficult nutritional conditions, the only food available for the patients was grated potato soup, which was administered to them almost like medicine, one tablespoon per person, three times a day. The portion of soup was increased each day...

The severe physical exhaustion of the former prisoners limited the possibilities for giving them injections. On one occasion, I received orders to give a sick former prisoner an intramuscular injection of *camphochina*. I could not carry it out, since she, like other patients, was suffering from complete muscular atrophy. In this situation, I went to the head physician, Dr. Józef Bellert, and informed him that I was unable to carry out the order for obvious reasons. Dr. Bellert lost his temper and chastised me, telling me that I did not know how to work. Among other things, he told me: "Who do they send here to work? They don't even know how to give injections...! I'll show you how to do it, nurse!" He hurried over to the patient and pulled back her blanket. When he saw what bad shape she was in, he apologized to me. I could see that he was moved. He left the room...

The PRC Camp Hospital in Oświęcim was independent, but cooperated closely with the Soviet army field hospital for former prisoners that was operating at the same time. The Soviet field hospitals were changed. Among the Soviet personnel, I remember Major Doctor Polakov and Dr. Zhilinska...

Major Dr. Polakov came to the buildings from time to time. He examined the patients, looked over their charts, and added his own remarks. In the block where I worked and in the other blocks, the nursing personnel included both PRC nurses and Soviet nurses and practical nurses. In each block, there were one or two (seldom three) PRC nurses, and several Soviet nurses. Ex-prisoners were a great help to us in maintaining cleanliness. As orderlies, they washed the floors, brought water, lighted the stoves, and carried out the corpses. In the block where

I worked, the active ex-prisoners included Aldo Ragazzi from Italy and two Yugoslavians whose names I did not know. Despite open tubercular lesions, one of the Yugoslavians performed all sorts of duties with exceptional zeal. Ex-prisoner physicians also worked with us.

During my time in Oświęcim, I worked in Blocks 12, 13, 22, and 24 in turn. In Block No. 24, the prisoners had better conditions. They were in two-person rooms on the second floor...

During the last two–three months before I left Oświęcim, the conditions for the ex-prisoner patients improved radically. The multi-tiered bunks were removed and the prisoners placed in regular single beds with clean sheets. There were no longer any shortages of medicine. The rooms were illuminated with electric lighting. Some of the sinks in the buildings were already serviceable. The toilets, however, continued to be closed, probably because they were damaged. For this reason, everyone continued to make use of the primitive latrines located between the blocks. These were open holes.

In the final phase of my stay in Oświęcim, that is, in May–July 1945, the office of the PRC hospital was located in the building of the former Auschwitz Concentration Camp administration building outside the camp fence, near the river Soła. The PRC doctors and nurses lived on the second floor of this building. This block was made of bare bricks, without stucco...

The results of the work by the PRC doctors and nurses are indicated by the proofs of gratitude shown to them by those... who left the hospital. With extraordinary gratitude, they thanked us for our care, and often invited us to their countries and families, leaving their addresses and photographs. The Italian whom I mentioned above, Aldo Ragazzi, gave me a personal invitation, as did his two Yugoslavian colleagues. I never made use of these invitations, and did not remain in touch with them...

At first, the mortality among the prisoners... was horrific. In a later period, this mortality diminished considerably, until in the end there were hardly any deaths at all. More and more ex-prisoners left the hospital each day. In general, special transports were organized for the discharged. They traveled by truck. On several occasions, special missions from abroad took ex-prisoners with them.

(1972)

Source: APMAB, Testimonies Fond, vol. 74, pp. 174–182.

No. 20
From an account by former child prisoner Ewa Krcz-Sieczka (camp number A-5116), probably deported from Hungary:

I am the adopted daughter of Józef and Karolina Krcz. I have borne the surname Krcz since the moment of the liberation of Birkenau Concentration Camp (January 27, 1945), that is, from the time when I was taken, as a small child, from the barracks of Birkenau. I do not know where I come from, when and where I was born, or which transport brought me to Auschwitz.

I know that, after the liberation of the Nazi Auschwitz-Birkenau camp in Oświęcim-Brzezinka, Stanisław Krcz (my foster brother) went to the barracks of Brzezinka and, from among the children there, chose me. I stayed from that time with the Krcz family, who adopted me. The father who adopted me died in 1955, and I am now under the care of my mother, Karolina Krcz.

I attended the Queen Hedwig elementary school in Oświęcim, and then the Konarski General Secondary School in Oświęcim. I passed my final school exams there in 1960 and, after passing the entrance examinations, enrolled as a student in the Dentistry Department of the Medical Faculty at the Medical Academy in Krakow...

My brother Stanisław Krcz... told me that, when he took me from the barracks of Brzezinka, he was told that I had arrived at the camp in a Hungarian transport.

From the time when I was in the camp, I have the camp number A-5116 tattooed on my left forearm. I remember the clothing in which I was taken from the camp. I wore high red leather shoes, a blue dress, and a coat in bright-colored and black stripes.

At some point in 1946, I was examined by an older physician in Bielsko-Biała. I do not know the name of that doctor...

Additionally, I know Lidia Rydzikowska, who was also taken as a child from the Birkenau camp, who now works as a technician at the Chemical Plant in Dwory...[18]

Source: APMAB, Testimonies Fond, vol. 12, pp. 127–128.

---

[18] Despite many years of searching, Ewa Krcz has never located her birth family.

No. 21
Stanisław Krcz on his foster sister Ewa:

In January 1945 – immediately after the liberation of Auschwitz – news went around that there was a sizeable group of orphan children in the camp who required care. As far as I remember, I went with several friends to the grounds of the former camp in Brzezinka on the third day after liberation... I went to the barracks where the little children were... I decided to take one of the children home... In the barracks was an older woman of about 50, the block supervisor... She showed me a little girl and said that the girl had arrived in the camp together with her parents and younger brother... She told me the name of the child – Ewa – and the last name, which I believe was Sztolc... Ewa's appearance and state indicated that the child was malnourished, sickly, and, above all, badly neglected. Ewa then had a large head, a large belly, which must have been swelling, and a large scab on her head, above her forehead... I carried little Ewa to our apartment in Kolejowa Street... My mother looked at Ewa and despaired over her appearance. She was afraid that the child wouldn't survive... She threw all her energy into saving her. She began with baths in various herbs and salts, and medicine. Ewa woke up crying every morning... The late Dr. Komraus looked very tenderly after Ewa and, seeing that she was a child from the camp, never accepted the fees due to him. Ewa's physical condition improved from one day to the next, but scars long remained in the child's mind. For a long time, Ewa was afraid of dogs. Even the tiniest lapdog sent her into nervous shock. At the sight of a dog, she burst out crying, ran away, and hid... She did not know how to play. On more than one occasion, I brought her some sort of toy, but all she ever did was look at it; later, she threw it aside and took no interest in it... The child's nervousness was burdensome, but it faded over time...

(1963)

Source: APMAB, Testimonies Fond, vol. 37, pp. 100–103.

II. Photographs

Photograph 1. The evacuation routes from Auschwitz were strewn with the corpses of prisoners. One of the victims of the evacuation.
APMAB, Neg. No. 405.

Photograph 2. An evacuation transport of Auschwitz prisoners at the moment of departure from Kolin train station in Bohemia, January 24, 1945. The photograph comes from a brief film made illegally by a Kolin resident, Jindøich Kremer, with a home movie camera.
APMAB, Neg. No. 20815/3.

Photograph 3. Some participants and eyewitness produced artistic represen-
tations of the "Death March" after the war. Zbigniew Otfinowski, a Krakow
artist who witnessed the evacuation of prisoners near Dzierżoniów in Lower
Silesia, painted this picture in 1946. APMAB, Neg. No. 14942, 1023/87.

Photograph 4. Among the many monuments commemorating the victims of the evacuation of Auschwitz, this one in Leszczyny-Rzędówka near Rybnik is notable for its expressive form. More than 300 Auschwitz prisoners died here or in the vicinity.
APMAB, Neg. No. 20695/4.

Photograph 5. SS men withdrawing from Auschwitz
demolished the crematoria and gas chambers.
APMAB, Neg. No. 1204.

Photograph 6. Withdrawing SS men set fire to warehouse barracks
in Birkenau containing the property of Jewish victims; the fire burned
for five days. APMAB, Neg. No. 942.

Photograph 7. Auschwitz was liberated on January 27, 1945. Former prisoners and Soviet soldiers attempted to reenact the moment for the film camera several weeks later. APMAB, Neg. No. 1243, 19583.

Photograph 8. The Soviet army medical service and the Polish Red Cross immediately came to the aid of the liberated Auschwitz prisoners.
APMAB, Neg. No. 554.

Photograph 9. A ward in the Polish Red Cross camp hospital in Oświęcim. Standing fourth from left is Sister Sylwina Chrapkowska, with the Polish Red Cross nurses Barbara Woźny and Michalina Prokopowicz next, and Sister Przemysława Uchyła first from right.
APMAB, Neg. No. 802.

Photograph 10. There were more then two hundred children among the patients of the Soviet field hospital and the Polish Red Cross hospital. Sister Tacjana Pożarowszczyk, who helped care for them, at rear.
APMAB, Neg. No. 21958/34.

Photograph 11. More than 230 Red Army soldiers died fighting to liberate the camp, the city of Oświęcim, and the vicinity. The grave of the fallen in Dąbrowskiego Street in Oświęcim.
APMAB, Neg. No. 21826.

Photograph 12. At the moment of the liberation of the camp, the bodies of about 600 prisoners, who had been shot or who died of starvation and exhaustion, were found.
APMAB, Neg. No. 547,828.

Photograph 13. The ceremonial funeral on February 28, 1945 of prisoners who were killed in the last days of the camp or who died shortly after liberation.
APMAB, Neg. No. 684, 19943.

Photograph 14. Brzezinka, February/March 1945. Former prisoners being transferred to brick buildings at the site of the Main Camp in Oświęcim.
APMAB, Neg. No. 19587.

Photograph 15. A group of former prisoners sets out for home.
APMAB, Neg. No. 19490.

Photograph 16. The staffs of the Soviet field hospitals and the Polish Red
Cross hospital at the liberated camp recorded their work together in nu-
merous photographs. This one was taken outside the former SS hospital.
From left: Major Polakov, Dr. Zdzisław Makomaski, Major Dr. Zhylinskaya
with Włodzimierz, the son of Polish Red Cross head nurse Genowefa
Przybysz, nurse Janina Stankiewicz (in the dark dress). In the second row:
Soviet political commissar Shayn, nurses Jadwiga Golec and Maria Rogoż,
and nurse Ewa Nowosielecka (in front of the window).
APMAB, Neg. No.19179.

Photograph 17. The Extraordinary State Commission of the USSR for the Investigation of German Crimes and the Commission for the Investigation of German Crimes in Poland conducted a thorough investigation of the crimes committed in Auschwitz. At left: the Polish commission at the ruins of Crematorium V in Birkenau; at right: a session of the Soviet commission, chaired by General Dr. Dymitr Kudriavtzev, in the office that previously belonged to Commandant Rudolf Höss. APMAB, Neg. No. 790, 21334/138.

Photograph 18. A young former prisoner in front of the Soviet forensic medicine commission. APMAB, Neg. No. 14333.

III. Documents

1. Decree of July 20, 1944 from the commander of the police and security service of the General Government on the evacuation and liquidation of prisons and compulsory labor camps for Jews. Similar guidelines were almost certainly followed during the evacuation and liquidation of Auschwitz:

Once again I must point out that the number of inmates in the Security Police and Security Service (Sipo u. SD) prisons must be reduced wherever possible. [...]

To the degree that the situation on the front makes it necessary, timely orders must be issued for the complete emptying of the prisons. Should an unforeseen development of the situation make it impossible to transport the prisoners, their liquidation is ordered, with the proviso that the bodies of those shot must be removed to the degree possible (burning, dynamiting buildings, etc.). In such a situation, the Jews employed in armaments factories or elsewhere must be dealt with in a similar way.

Under no circumstances should a situation arise in which either prisoners or Jews are liberated or fall into enemy hands, regardless of whether this is resistance movement bands or the Red Army[19].

Source: Reimund Schnabel, *Macht ohne Moral. Eine Dokumentation über die SS*, Frankfurt am Main 1957, p. 459 (Nuremberg document L-53).

---

[19] The commander of the police and security service in the Radom District cited this decree in July 21, 1944 orders to the local unit in Tomaszów Mazowiecki.

2. Excerpts from December 21, 1944 guidelines by Upper Silesia *Gauleiter*, *Oberpräsident*, and Reich Defense Commissar Fritz Bracht on the evacuation of civilians, conscript laborers, POWs, and prisoners, including those from Auschwitz.

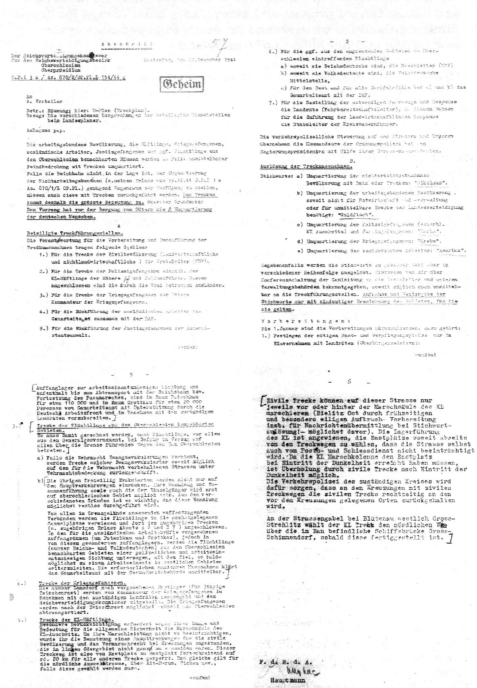

Source: Original in the Military Historical Museum in Prague, microfilm in AP-MAB No. 893, pp. 58–69.

Translation:

Copy

Katowice, December 21, 1944

Commissioner for the Defense of the Reich
For the Reich Defense District
Upper Silesia
Office of the Chief District Administrator
O.P.I 3a / Az. 870/2/OP.Pl. L 554/44 g　　　　　**SECRET**

To
See: recipients

Concerning: evacuation, map (plan for the route of the columns).
In reference to: various meetings of the offices concerned with the township planner

Enclosed:
[excerpts]

In the face of the imminent danger from the enemy, civilians under labor obligation, prisoners, POWs, foreign workers, workers, prisoners subject to judicial procedures, and refugees from the areas bordering Upper Silesia will be relocated in columns.

If the railroads are unable to provide a sufficient quantity of cars for the purpose of relocating persons who are not under a labor obligation (see my directive O.P.I 3 a Az. 870/1/L OP.Pl., of December 19, 1944), they too must be conducted in columns. The greatest significance is therefore attached to the columns. The most important principle is: The relocation of German civilians takes priority over the protection of property.

[...]

5. Columns of concentration camp prisoners.

Special vigilance is required in view of the length and overall significance for security of the Auschwitz Concentration Camp marching columns. So as not to impede the progress of the march, they have the right to use the main civilian routes and the marching right-of-way at intersections when these cannot be bypassed on the left bank of the Oder. This route will be systematically sealed off from all other columns in segments about 20 km. in length, from one stopping place to another. This also applies to the northern bypass route through Stary Bieruń, Tychy, etc., if it proves necessary.

In all cases, civilian columns may march on these routes only ahead of or behind the marching column from Auschwitz (Bielsko East, at especially high speed, with information conveyed by password! – with as much prior notice as possible). The concentration camp administration has been ordered to choose stopping places off the road, as far as possible from the route of the [civilian] columns, so that the same road will not be burdened by the presence of supervisory personnel or armed escorts. Since the marching column from the concentration camp must arrive at the designated stopping place by nightfall, it is possible for civilian marching columns to overtake it during the hours of darkness.

The police directing road traffic in a given administrative area will take care that, in cases of intersection with passing civilian columns, the latter will be stopped ahead of time in the localities just before the crossings. [...]

Approved
(illegible)
Hauptmann

3. January 2, 1945 letter from Major Boesenberg (liaison officer of the commander of SS and police in Breslau – now Wrocław) to commandant Eichberg of the POW camp in Cieszyn on changes to the plans approved 12 days earlier for routes by which prisoners of the Auschwitz sub-camps in Jaworzno, Siemianowice, and Sosnowiec would be evacuated on foot, with a map of the new evacuation routes.

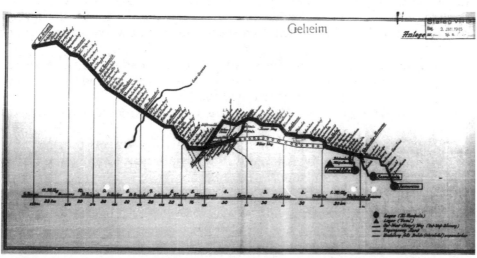

Source: Original in the Military Historical Museum in Prague, microfilm in AP-MAB No. 893, pp. 178, 180.

Translation:

Breslau, January 2, 1945
Sternstraße 32/34
Bö/We

**Higher Commander of SS and Police "Südost"
in the Districts of Lower Silesia and Upper Silesia
and in Defense District VIII
Liaison Officer**

SECRET

**Herr
Oberstleutnant* Eichberg
M. – Main Camp VIII B**

Cieszyn, Upper Silesia
Concerning: new marching routes for Jaworzno, Sosnowitz, and
Laurahütte concentration camps, and also for the VoMi [Volksdeutsche
Mittelstelle – Ethnic Germans' Welfare Office – trans.] camps, and pris-
oners of the Commandant of Security Police in Katowice.

In reference to: meeting at the office of Commissioner Ziegler, Katowice,
December 21, 1944.

I enclose the map of the new marching routes for the above-men-
tioned units within the territory of the Higher Commander of SS and
Police "Südost", while also pointing out that, as has been decided, the
POWs from the Sosnowiec camps will march together with the prisoners
from the concentration camps, and persons from the Ethnic Germans'
Welfare Office (VoMi).

In the correspondence with reference number OP. I. 3a / OP. PL./L.
Az.: 870/2/519/44 g, dated December 21, 1944, as sent to you in the
meantime by Commissioner Ziegler, this marching route is still marked
in the version from before the joint meeting in Katowice on December
21, 1944.

The Higher Commander of SS and Police "Südost" has in the meantime expressed his approval of the new route, as indicated on the map
enclosed by me, together with the POWs.

Commissioner Ziegler in Katowice has been informed of everything to
this effect.

The route alternate route marked in pink may also be taken into
consideration for the POWs should it prove impossible to cross the bridge
in Oderwinkel [Kąty Opolskie].

You should take the final point of this letter into consideration when
issuing instructions to the POW camps concerned.

Please confirm the receipt of this letter.

Authorized signature
Security Police Major
(illegible)

Enclosed: Map

Oberstleutnant* – lieutenant colonel

Map of the major pedestrian evacuation routes of KL Auschwitz prisoners in January 1945

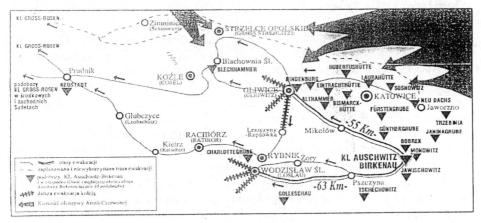

Edited by Andrzej Strzelecki
Design by Paweł Warchoł

4. Beginning of a report on the evacuation of prisoners from Upper Silesia. Drawn up on February 1, 1945 in Neisse (now Nysa) by Procurator General Haffner for Reich Justice Minister Otto Thierack.

The evolution of the situation in Upper Silesia is apparent in today's joint report, to which I refer. Rapidly developing events cannot fail to influence the transport of prisoners. The planned marching routes are partially unusable because the streets are blocked or within the range of enemy activity. The blocking of the streets results from the partial evacuation of 1,500,000 civilians from the endangered areas in marching columns. Unforeseen motor vehicle columns are traveling in a westward and southwestward direction on the few main roads. In addition, there are withdrawing columns of Wehrmacht and Police. Yet almost 50,000 male and female Auschwitz concentration camp prisoners and thousands of English and Soviet POWs are being sent along these same roads. I have been informed that, of columns numbering 3,000 POWs, 1,000 arrive at the destination. In the complete confusion that prevails on the roads, which is made worse by enemy air attacks, I regard this as completely possible. There are no words to describe the scenes occurring before our eyes. The road is strewn with the countless bodies of the dead, fallen horses, and overturned vehicles.

The situation became greatly exacerbated from January 20 to 23. Namely, according to information from the head of Security Police, things reached the inconceivable point where 8,000 to 9,000 concentration camp prisoners could not be transported and were left without supervision.

Dr. Haffner

Source: APMAB, D-RF-3/RSHA/160, pp. 45–49, photocopy.

5. Report from the commandant of the gendarmerie in Miedźna near Pszczyna, January 19, 1945, on the discovery of 39 corpses of prisoners murdered during the Auschwitz evacuation march.

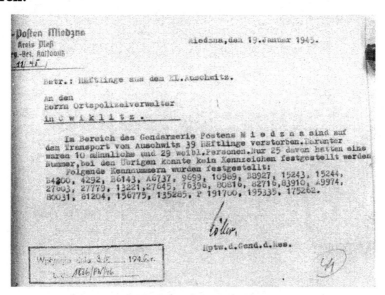

Source: APMAB, Materials Fond, vol. 43, Mat./595; Microfilm No. 1540/16.

Translation:

Miedźna, January 19, 1945

Miedźna
Pszczyna (Pleß) Township
Katowice District
11/45

Concerning: prisoners from Auschwitz Concentration Camp
To:
Chief of the Police Post
in Ćwiklice

39 prisoners died within the area of the Gendarmerie Post in Miedźna during the transport from Auschwitz. Among them 10 men and 29 women. Only 25 of them had numbers, and no markings could be found in the cases of the others.

The following numbers were noted:
B4200, 4292, B6143, A6737, 9699, 10989, B8927, 15243, 15244, 27603, 27779, 13221, 27645, 76396, 80816, 82716, 83910, A9974, 80031, 81204, 156775, P 191700, 195335, 175262.

Chief of the Gendarmerie Station
(illegible)

6. Unofficial handwritten list of the camp numbers of prisoners who died during the evacuation and were buried in Wilchwy near Wodzisław Śląski.

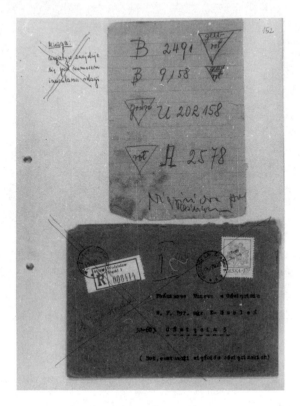

Source: APMAB, Testimonies Fond, vol. 89 p. 152; Microfilm No. 1283/152.

7. Protocol from the exhumation of 23 corpses of Auschwitz prisoners put to death in Kałków, Olsztyn region, in January 1945, during the Auschwitz evacuation march.

Protocol

Forensic Commission convened in Kałków on November 12, 1947 to exhume the corpses of political prisoners from a mass grave.

Present: Municipal magistrate from Nysa Włodzimierz Wojtowicz, Regional Court Procurator from Nysa (with temporary seat in Prudnik) Stefan Markowski; law clerk Juliusz Budyn, expert witnesses Dr. Marian Wontor township physician, Dr. Julian Sewerski municipal physician in Nysa, in the presence of People's Militia commandant in Nysa township 2nd. Lt. Antoni Kręźeł, the township Security Bureau representative and local Kałków township burgess Roman Gablak, French mission consisting of Capt. Carié and interpreter in attendance.

After arriving in the locality of Kałków the forensic commission followed directions from Kałków township burgess Roman Gablak to a wooded site approx. 2 km. from the locality of Kałków, where the burgess showed the forensic commission the location of the mass grave at the edge of the woods. The mass grave was already partially excavated with the top layer of soil dug away and human remains visible in the form of scattered bones and skulls, and fragments of rotten clothing. The exhumation of the remains began. In view of the total decomposition of the corpses, only 23 human skulls were exhumed, of which 2 skulls were declared by the medical experts to have been broken by a blunt instrument; rotten bits of clothing were also removed, and consisted exclusively of camp clothing (striped garments).

It was noted that the sleeves and legs of the trousers were tied with wire, and that wire was also used in several cases instead of belts, to hold the trousers up. It was noted that wooden clogs were the predominant type of footwear, and several pairs of sandal-type footwear were found, consisting only of a wooden sole and toe straps; in one case, three sets of clothing were noted, one worn over the other. During the examination of the clothing, camp insignia in the form of rectangular strips of cloth were found sewn to the blouses and jackets, on which there were superimposed red-yellow colored triangles[20], and camp numbers. On two insignia, the letter F was clearly visible, and two others

---

[20] Triangles – cloth insignia sewn on camp garments. The color denoted the prisoner category. Yellow was for Jewish prisoners and red for political prisoners. Until mid-1944, the triangles for Jewish prisoners were sewn in the shape of a Star of David; afterwards a rectangular yellow stripe was placed over the triangle [ed.].

bore the letters H and A, respectively[21]. The following numbers were legible on the corpses: 168283, 200707, 77075, 170126, 178253, 176679, 176765, 177334, 176613, 176765, 177800, 170082, and a number ending in 991. In the pockets of the clothing were found newspapers, notes, and scraps of paper, and particularly newspapers in French and Czech, a book in German, one postcard with the address "Konzentrationslager Auschwitz", one letter in French, a label with the inscription "Konzentrationslager Auschwitz", and other illegible notes.

The above-mentioned insignia and writings were placed in the attached envelopes.

After the conclusion of the exhumation, the local administrative authorities, that is, the burgess of Kałków, was instructed to place the remains of the corpses in several caskets and to bury them in the local cemetery, which was carried out according to a telephone report from Kałków, with the details that the remains of the exhumed corpses were placed in three caskets and buried in the cemetery in Kałków, with the local priest and residents in attendance.

(illegible signature)

Source: APMAB, Other Fonds (IZ 72/1), pp. 16–17 (copy). Original in the collections of the Institute of National Remembrance (IPN), Ko. 568/47.

---

[21] The initial letter of the German name of a prisoner's nationality was indicated in ink on the triangle. F (Franzose) could refer to deportees from France, and H from the Netherlands (*Holländer*), while A (if it was an A) would indicate a Jewish prisoner deported to Auschwitz after mid-May 1944, when new series of numbers, including one beginning with A, were introduced for Jewish prisoners because the numbers from the "general series" were growing so large as to be unwieldy [ed.].

8. First page of a list of names of former prisoners treated in the 6th ward of Soviet field hospital No. 2020, on the Auschwitz grounds.

9. Partial list of names of children cared for by the Polish Red Cross in Brzezinka in February 1945, including twins who were the victims of Dr. Mengele's experiments.

POLSKI CZERWONY KRZYŻ

W y k a z

dzieci i matek, znajdujących się w Obozie Oświęcim-Birkenau, zebrany przez dr.Rollerta w dniu 9 lutego 1945 r.

Blok 2.

Lp.	Nazwisko i Imię	Numer	Wiek	Miejscowość	Narodowość
1.	Birenowajg Eiuta	A 27622	7	Starachowice	polska
2.	Projek Moniuš	A 19947	2	Radom	"
3.	Bolinowska Gizella	A 27649	14	Łódź	"
4.	Balter Perla	A 16862	12	Ostrowiec	"
5.	Paskowa Zina		2		ruska
6.	Fekete Wilmoss	A 12089	7	Silad Nadfelen	węgierska
7.	Fekete Belo	A 7040	7	" "	"
8.	Kraönanski Iwan	B 14156	10	Bratislava	słowacka
9.	Kraub Hauka	73492	5	Praga	Czechosł.
10.	Kraub Ewa	73493	5	Praga	"
11.	Burger Toni	B 13987	11	Trebisof	Słow.
12.	Burger Franciszek	B 13986	6	"	"
13.	Hamburger Julius	B 14101	7	Bratislava	"
14.	Fuks Arpat	B 14054	7	Nitra	"
15.	Bucal Lilianna	76484	7	Fiume	Italia
16.	Neuman Juraj	B 14213	10	Bratislava	Słowacja
17.	Blumowa Vera	A 26847	11	Seczowce	"
18.	Feldbauerowa Marianna	A 26919	13	Bratislava	Słowacja
19.	Neumanowa Erika	A 27059	7	Sznaszów	Słowacja
20.	Neumanowa Judita	A 27060	6	"	"
21.	Diamont Ewa	A 26677	12	Budapest	Węgry
22.	Braumowa Judita	A 26840	11	Michalowce	Słowacja
23.	Alichow Brygida		5		Niemcy
24.	Binet Gaszpar	B 14005	6	Kireszkujwar	Węgry
25.	Binet Usza	B 14006	5	"	"
26.	Bucai Aleksander	76483	5	Fiume	Italia
27.	Projek Rajala	A 15687	30	Radom	Polska
28.	Birenowajg Basia	A 27777	32	Starachowice	"
29.	Balter Perla	A 16861	41	Ostrowiec	"

Source: APMAB, PCK/12, p. 111, Microfilm No. 1115/111.

10. List of names of former prisoners in a repatriation transport from Oświęcim to Ostrava, Czechoslovakia, in July 1945.

POLSKI CZERWONY KRZYŻ
Szpital Obozowy
w Oświęcimiu

Отправляются
в Моравскую Остраву 13. VII 45

тяжело больные лежачие.

1 Сапсико Виктория
2 Розеляр Матильда
3 Кокер юдита
4 Розенберг Ина
5 Де Рай Эдвард

Завед

Бр Беллерт.

Завтра завтра приедут
за ходячими больными.

Source: APMAB, PCK/12, p. 14, Microfilm No. 1115/14.

11. Certificate issued by the Polish Red Cross hospital administration at the Auschwitz grounds and the provisional city council in Oświęcim to Dr. Paulina Szpolańska, former prisoner in the Łódź ghetto and Auschwitz Concentration Camp.

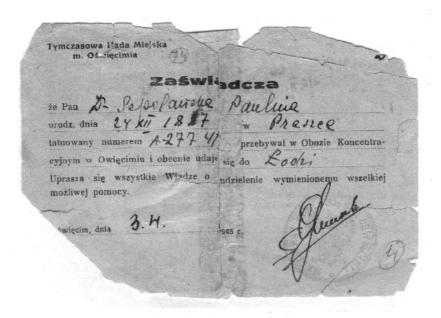

Source: APMAB, Other Fonds (IZ-13/14), pp. 74, 77, Inventory No. 158242.

12. Card identifying nurse Joanna Jakobi as a member of the staff at the Polish Red Cross hospital on the Auschwitz grounds.

Source: APMAB, PCK/22, p. 21, Microfilm No. 1118/21.

13. Certificate confirming that Dr. Bolesław Urbański worked as a doctor at the Polish Red Cross Camp Hospital in Oświęcim.

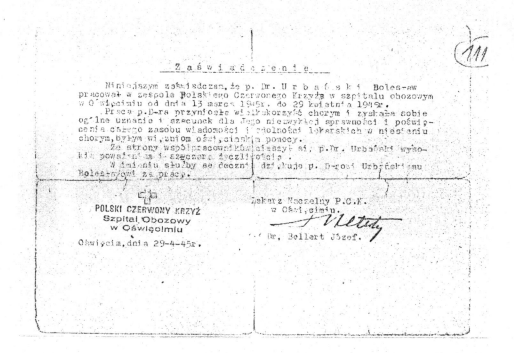

Source: APMAB, PCK/17, p. 111, Microfilm No. 1117/111.

14. Military pass issued to Dr. Bolesław Urbański for a three-day trip from Oświęcim to Krakow.

Source: APMAB, PCK/17, p. 110, Microfilm No. 1117/110.

15. Inscriptions by former prisoners from France and the USSR in the diary of Polish Red Cross nurse Michalina Prokopowicz of Oświęcim, thanking her for caring for them at the hospital on the grounds of the former camp.

Je suis heureux de pouvoir écrire combien nous avons été satisfait, non seulement de ton aide, mais surtout de l'ambiance que tu as créé chez nous.

le 28-4-1945

Дорогая Михалина!
Ваше внимание и заботу ко
мне, в дни моей болезни,
Я всегда буду вспоминать
с благодарностью.
        Жора.
г. Освенцим   1/III-45.

Source: АРМАВ, PCK/26, Inventory No. 167895.

16. **First three pages of a protocol of the Main Commission
for the Investigation of German Crimes in Poland, dated May
25, 1945, on the state of health of former Auschwitz prisoners
in the Polish Red Cross Camp Hospital in Oświęcim.**

O d p i s.

P r o t o k ó ł

Działo się w Oświęcimiu w czasie od 11 do 25 maja 1945 r. Sędzia
Śledczy w Krakowie Jan Sehn, Członek Głównej Komisji Badania
Zbrodni Niemieckich w Polsce dokonał na wniosek, w obecności
i przy współudziale Członka tejże Komisji Prokuratora Edwarda
Pęchalskiego w trybie art. 254 w związku z art 123 Kodeksu Po-
stępowania Karnego oględzin szpitala byłego obozu koncentracyjnego w Oświęcimiu i znajdujących się w tymże szpitalu chorych,
przyczym okazało się co następuje: - - - - - - - - - - - - - - -
Szpital mieści się w sześciu blokach obozu koncentracyjnego w Oświęcimiu, nazywanego w urzędowej korespondencji niemieckiej K.L.
Auschwitz I /Stammlager Auschwitz/, oznaczonych numerami 12, 13,
14, 22, 23 i 24. Są to budynki murowane, jednopiętrowe. W szpitalu znajduje się 388 chorych, byłych więźniów, spisanych w załą-
czonej liście według numerów bloków z podaniem nazwisk, dat uro-
dzenia, numeru więźnia, daty przybycia do obozu w Oświęcimiu,
wyznania i przynależności państwowej. /Załącznik 1, obejmujący
16 stron./ -
Wszyscy chorzy są niedożywieni, wychudzeni, większość obłożnie
chora pozostaje w łóżkach. Według wyjaśnienia lekarzy szpitalnych
chorzy ci cierpią na gruźlicę, pleuritis exsudativa, furunkulozę,
niedomogi i wady serca, odmrożenia, egzemy na tle awitaminozy,
distrofię alimentarną i inne choroby, wywołane i spowodowane wa-
runkami życia obozowego. -
Dla zilustrowania stanu i wyglądu chorych poddane zostały oglę-
dzinom ciała i sfotografowane przez przybranego fotografa Insty-
tutu Ekspertyz Sądowych w Krakowie, Stanisława Łuczkę, następujące
osoby, przebywające na różnych blokach: - - - - - - - - - - - - -

1. Ewa M ü h l r a d, urodzona 13.X. 1924 r. w Ujpest na Węgrzech,
narodowości i przynależności państwowej węgierskiej, wyznania
mojżeszowego, studentka, przybyła do obozu w Oświęcimiu 12.VII
1944 r.,gdzie otrzymała numer więzienny A 13160. – – – – – – –
Według oświadczenia Ewy Mühlrad, przybyła ona do obozu w Oświęcimiu w stanie zdrowym, a do szpitala przyjętą została 20.XI.
1944 r.z powodu biegunki i żółtaczki.Obecnie znajduje się na
bloku nr.14, a w załączonym spisie chorych figuruje pod numerem bieżącym 211. –
Chorą demonstrował obecny przy oględzinach lekarz bloku 14
dr Zdzisław Makomaski z Krakowa,który na podstawie historii
choroby i własnej obserwacji chorej oświadczył, iż Ewa Mühlrad
dotknięta jest chorobą, nazywaną przez lekarzy dystrophia alimentaris. Według terminologji lekarzy sowieckich,opartej na
doświadczeniach z okresu oblężenia Leningradu, jest to dystrophia alimentaris III gradus. Chora ta przy wzroście 156 cm.
waży obecnie 30 kg. Przed aresztowaniem ważyła 55 kg. W obec-
nym stanie chora jest całkiem przytomna i zdolna do składania
świadomych oświadczeń. – – – – – – – – – – – – – – – – – – –
Do protokółu załączono odpis historii choroby Ewy Mühlrad jako załącznik nr 2 oraz dwa zdjęcia fotograficzne, oznaczone
w załączniku nr 6, jako fotografie nr 1 i 1 A. – – – – – – – –
2. Klara C h e ł m i c k a, urodzona 10.X.1914 r. w Meklenburgu,
córka Jana i Marii, narodowości i przynależności państwowej
polskiej, wyznania rzymsko-katolickiego, gospodyni, przybyła
do obozu w Oświęcimiu 15. V. 1943 r., gdzie otrzymała numer
więzienny 44884. –
Według oświadczenia Klary Chełmickiej, aresztowana ona została w Łęczycy i przetransportowana do obozu w Oświęcimiu w stanie zdrowym. Do szpitala obozowego przyjęta została w listo-

-3-

3

padzie 1943 r. z powodu ogólnego osłabienia i upadku sił. Obecnie znajduje się na bloku nr 14, a w załączonym spisie chorych
wymieniona jest pod numerem bieżącym 159. - - - - - - - - -
Chorą demonstrował obecny przy oględzinach lekarz na bloku 14
dr Zdzisław Makomaski z Krakowa, który oświadczył, że stan chorej jest ciężki, że jednak jest ona przytomna i zdolna do składania świadomych oświadczeń. Według wyjaśnienia tegoż lekarza,
opartego na historii choroby i jego osobistej obserwacji chorej, Klara Chełmicka dotknięta jest chorobą dystrophia alimentaris III gradus oraz w wysokim stopniu rozwiniętą gruźlicą z
powstałymi w związku z tym otwartymi ranami skóry. Lekarz o-
kreślił wzrost chorej na 155 - 160 cm., a wagę na około 25 kg.
Z historii choroby wynika, iż Chełmicka przed aresztowaniem
ważyła 75 kg. -
Do protokółu załączono odpis historii choroby Klary Chełmickiej, jako załącznik nr 3 i dwa jej zdjęcia fotograficzne, o-
znaczone w załączniku nr 6, jako fotografje nr 2 i 2 A. - - -
3. Janette A p a r i z i o, urodzona 30. IX. 1903 r. w Rosji,
córka Samuela Spiro i Katarzyny White, narodowości i przynależności państwowej angielskiej, wyznania mojżeszowego, mę-
żatka, przybyła do obozu w Oświęcimiu 2. VI. 1944 r., gdzie
otrzymała numer więzienny A 7180. - - - - - - - - - - - - - -
Według oświadczenia Janette Aparizio, rodzina jej przebywała
początkowo w Rosji. W roku 1905 z powodu pogromu żydów w Rosji wyjechali Spirowie do Anglji i tam się osiedlili. Ojciec
jej zmarł w 56 roku życia na serce, a matka w 54 roku życia
na raka żołądka. Z czterech jej braci jeden zginął podczas
wojny światowej, a trzej pozostali przebywają obecnie w Lon-
dynie. Wyszła zamąż za obywatela angielskiego, pochodzącego
z Hiszpanii. Aresztowana została w roku 1939 przy usiłowaniu

Source: APMAB, Höss Trial, vol. 9, pp. 1–3, Microfilm No. 203/1–3.

Translation:

True Copy

Protocol

In Oświęcim, in the period from May 11 to 25, 1945, Investigating Judge Jan Sehn, Member of the Main Commission for the Investigation of German Crimes in Poland, at the request, in the presence, and with the participation of Prosecutor Edward Pęchalski, a Member of said Commission, under the procedures of article 254 in connection with article 123 of the Code of Criminal Procedure, did perform an examination of the hospital in the former concentration camp in Oświęcim and the patients found in that hospital, with findings as follows:

The hospital is located in six blocks of the concentration camp in Oświęcim, called in official German correspondence K.L. Auschwitz I (Stammlager Auschwitz), designated by the numbers 12, 13, 14, 22, 23, and 24. These are two-story brick buildings. 388 patients, former prisoners, are found in the hospital, entered on the attached list according to the numbers of the blocks with names, dates of birth, prisoner numbers, dates of arrival at the camp in Oświęcim, religious faith, and citizenship (Attachment 1, comprising 16 pages).

All the patients are malnourished, emaciated, and the majority of them are bedridden. According to statements by the physicians at the hospital, these patients are suffering from tuberculosis, pleuritis exsudativa, phurunculosis, cardiac insufficiency and defects, frostbite, eczema due to vitamin deficiency, alimentary dystrophy, and other diseases brought about and caused by the conditions of life in the camp.

To illustrate the condition and appearance of the patients, the following persons, hospitalized in various blocks, were subjected to a physical examination and photographed by the photographer recommended by the Institute of Forensic Science in Krakow, Stanisław Łuczka:

1. Ewa Mühlrad, born Oct. 13, 1924 in Ujpest, Hungary, of Hungarian nationality and citizenship, of the Mosaic [Jewish – trans.] religion, student, arrived in the camp in Oświęcim on July 12, 1944, where she obtained prison number A 13160.

According a statement by Ewa Mühlrad, she arrived at the camp in Oświęcim in healthy condition, and was admitted to the hospital on Nov. 20, 1944 because of diarrhea and jaundice. She is now in Block 14, and she figures on the attached list of patients as number 211.

Dr. Zdzisław Makomaski of Krakow, the doctor of Block 14, presented the patient and stated, on the basis of the medical history and his own observation of the patient, that Ewa Mühlrad is suffering from the disease referred to by doctors as dystrophia alimentaris.

According to the terminology of the Soviet physicians, based on experience from the time of the siege of Leningrad, this is dystrophia alimentaris III gradus. The patient is 156 cm. [5'1"] tall and weighs 30 kg. [66 lbs.]. Before arrest, she weighed 55 kg. [121 lbs.]. In her present condition, the patient is fully aware and capable of making conscious statements.

Attached to the protocol is the medical history of Ewa Mühlrad as attachment 2, and two photographs, designated in attachment 6 as photographs No. 1 and 1 A.

2. Klara Chełmicka, born Oct. 10, 1914 in Mecklemburg, daughter of Jan and Maria, of Polish nationality and citizenship, the Roman-Catholic religion, domestic, arrived in the camp in Oświęcim on May 15, 1943, where she obtained prison number 44884.

According a statement by Klara Chełmicka, she was arrested in Łęczyca and transported to the camp in Oświęcim in healthy condition. She was admitted to the camp hospital in November 1943 because of general atrophy and loss of strength. She is now in Block 14, and she figures on the attached list of patients as number 159.

Dr. Zdzisław Makomaski of Krakow, the doctor of Block 14, presented the patient and stated that the patient is in serious condition, that she is nevertheless aware and capable of making conscious statements. According to the explanation by this doctor, based on the medical history and his personal observation of the patient, Klara Chełmicka is suffering from the disease of dystrophia alimentaris III gradus and very advanced tuberculosis, with open skin lesions arising as a result. The doctor defined the height of the patient as from 155 to 160 cm. [5'1" to 5'3"], and her weight as approximately 25 kg. [55 lbs.]. The medical history indicates that, before arrest, Chełmicka weighed 75 kg. [165 lbs.].

Attached to the protocol is the medical history of Klara Chełmicka as Attachment 3, and two photographs of her, designated in Attachment 6 as photographs No. 2 and 2 A.

3. Janette Aparizio, born Sept. 30, 1903 in Russia, the daughter of Samuel Spiro and Katarzyna White, of English nationality and citizenship, of the Mosaic [Jewish – trans.] religion, married, arrived in the camp in Oświęcim on June 2, 1944, where she obtained camp number A 7180.

According a statement by Janette Aparizio, her family was initially living in Russia. In 1905, as a result of the pogrom of the Jews in Russia, the Spiros emigrated to England and settled there. Her father died in the 56th year of his life of heart disease, and her mother in the 54th year of her life of stomach cancer. Of her four brothers, one died during the world war, and the remaining three are living at present in London. She married an English citizen who comes from Spain. She was arrested in 1939 when attempting [...]

Annexes

Biographical Sketches of the Authors of Accounts

BATOR, ZOFIA, nee **Stępień,** born June 3, 1920 in Radom. Belonged to the Gray Ranks (a clandestine Polish scouting organization) during the occupation. Arrested in Radom on October 16, 1942, and imprisoned in Auschwitz on March 3 of the following year. Camp number 37255. Assigned at first to external labor details, later sent to the penal company in Budy. After surviving typhus, worked in the hospital as a "buffer" (cleaner); later transferred to the knitting labor detail (*Stickerei*), bread room (*Brotkammer*), and the SS kitchen, where she labored until evacuation. In Auschwitz, she clandestinely painted portraits of fellow prisoners, including Mala Zimetbaum. Evacuated to Ravensbrück Concentration Camp in January 1945, and later to the Neustadt-Glewe sub-camp, where Soviet soldiers liberated her on May 2, 1945.

EHRLICH, RUDOLF, born in Stalec, near Tabor (Czechoslovakia), on June 15, 1902. Imprisoned in the Theresienstadt ghetto from June 1, 1942 to October 18, 1944. Deported from there to Auschwitz, arriving on October 21. After two days in Birkenau, sent to the "Fürstengrube" sub-camp near Mysłowice as a slave laborer in a coal mine there; worked underground until January 18, 1945. After the SS abandoned the sub-camp, the prisoners who remained there received help from local civilians. Ehrlich was treated in hospitals in Mysłowice and Oświęcim.

GRADOWSKI, ZAŁMEN, born in Suwałki, probably in 1910. Deported to Auschwitz, along with his entire family, from a transit camp in Kiełbasin, near Grodno, on December 8, 1942. The rest of his family was sent to the gas chambers on arrival; Załmen Gradowski was assigned to the *Sonderkommando*. While a member of the *Sonderkommando*, he took notes and buried the notes near Crematorium III. He took an active part in preparations for the mutiny by the *Sonderkommando*, and died in the course of the rebellion on October 7, 1944.

KONIECZNA, IRENA, born in Poznań on October 7, 1905. Graduated from medical school there in 1932 and was a practicing gynecologist. Arrested in Inowrocław in November 1939; expelled after release to

Starachowice, where she joined the underground resistance movement. Detained during mass arrests in Starachowice on August 21, 1943 and deported to Auschwitz II-Birkenau in a transport from Radom two days later; received camp number 55037. Worked in the camp hospital and was in charge of the gynecologist's office that opened in the fall of 1944. Worked selflessly to help prisoners who required long-term treatment. Refused to carry out abortions ordered by the *Lagerarzt* (camp physician). Helped sick children. After the evacuation in January 1945, remained behind to care for sick and exhausted prisoners. Worked first in the Soviet field hospital, and next in the PRC hospital.

KOPROWSKA, WANDA, born in Sosnowiec on August 7, 1909. Deported to Auschwitz on February 12, 1943, in a transport of political prisoners from Silesia. Initially imprisoned in Block No. 2a, which was at the disposal of the investigative jail in Mysłowice; transferred to the women's camp in Birkenau on March 5 and given camp number 37573. In the Budy sub-camp from April 4, 1943 until April 22, 1944, laboring in the fields and at the demolition of houses whose owners had been expelled. After returning to Birkenau, labored in the outside labor details that drained and dredged ponds, weeded, and peeled vegetables in the "*szelkuchnia*". Evacuated to Ravensbrück in October 1944.

KUCHARSKA, ZOFIA, nee **Lutomska,** born in Warsaw on December 12, 1916. Arrested on May 17, 1941, and deported to Auschwitz II-Birkenau from Warsaw on July 16, 1943. Camp number 49999. Initially assigned to various kinds of field labor in outside labor details. Fell ill, and assigned after recovery to work as a nurse in the hospital in sector BIIe, the so-called "Gypsy Camp". Avoided evacuation in January 1945 and stayed behind until liberation.

MANDELBAUM, HENRYK, born in Olkusz on October 15, 1922. Forced to settle in the ghetto in Dąbrowa Górnicza, along with his family, in 1940; after liquidation of that ghetto, sent to the Sosnowiec ghetto. His parents were sent to Auschwitz and died in the gas chamber. Remained in hiding until April 1943, arrested when someone informed to the Gestapo. After being held for a year in the Sosnowiec prison, sent to Auschwitz on April 23, 1944; given camp number 181970. Assigned to the *Sonderkommando* in July. Escaped in Jastrzębie Zdrój during the evacuation march in January 1945. Testified at the trial of Rudolf Höss. Frequently met with young people to talk about the crimes he witnessed. Died in 2008.

PAISIKOVIC, DOV, born in Velky Rakovec (then Hungary, now Ukraine) on April 1, 1924.
Sent to the ghetto in Munkacs (Hungary) on April 15, deported from there to Auschwitz II-Birkenau in May 1944; camp number A-3076. Assigned to the *Sonderkommando*. After evacuation in January 1945,

imprisoned in Mauthausen and later in the Ebensee sub-camp. Liberated there by American troops in May.

STEINHARDT, ABRAHAM, in Auschwitz from 1942 [?]. Worked in the labor detail that demolished the homes of Polish farmers expelled from the vicinity (*Abbruchkommando*). Evacuated in January 1945 to Gross-Rosen and then to Bergen-Belsen; liberated by British soldiers on April 15, 1945.

TABACZYŃSKI, JÓZEF, born in Myszków on October 26, 1915; camp number 114780. Deported to Auschwitz from the prison in Sosnowiec in February 1943. Assigned three months later to Auschwitz III-Monowitz; labored on excavation work during the construction of the Buna chemical plant; also worked in the food stores and camp kitchen. Sent after evacuation in January 1945 to Dora Concentration Camp, later to its Erlich sub-camp, and finally to the Heinkel plant near Berlin. Liberated by American soldiers during the evacuation of that plant on May 3, 1945.

TARASIEWICZ, WANDA, nee **Błachowska,** born in Brzozów on August 1, 1920. Lived in Nowy Targ during the occupation and joined the underground Tatra Confederation. Imprisoned in Tarnów after the organization was broken up in early 1942; deported to Auschwitz in the first transport of Polish women prisoners on April 27, 1942. Assigned camp number 6884. Labored in the SS laundry. Escaped during evacuation in Brzeźce near Pszczyna, and returned home to Nowy Targ when the fighting ended. Active member of organizations that aided former concentration camp prisoners and disabled veterans after the war. Frequently held meetings with young people. Died on November 17, 2001.

Timeline of Important Events in Auschwitz Concentration Camp

April 1940 – Heinrich Himmler ordered the founding of a concentration camp, which would be built and expanded by prisoner labor, in old army barracks in Oświęcim.

May 4, 1940 – Rudolf Höss is officially named commandant of Konzentrationslager Auschwitz.

June 14, 1940 – the first transport of Polish political prisoners arrives from the prison in Tarnów (728 men).

July 6, 1940 – Tadeusz Wiejowski, a Pole, is the first prisoner to escape. In reprisal, all prisoners are subjected to a 20-hour-long punitive roll call.

November 22, 1940 – the first executions by shooting (40 Polish prisoners).

March 1, 1941 – the first visit to Auschwitz by Heinrich Himmler, who orders that the camp be expanded to hold 30 thousand prisoners, that a new camp to hold 100 thousand POWs be built on the site of the village of Brzezinka, and that 10 thousand prisoners be supplied to the IG Farbenindustrie company for the construction of a plant in Monowice-Dwory on the outskirts of Oświęcim.

April 23, 1941 – for the first time, 10 hostages were sentenced to death by starvation in reprisal for an escape by a prisoner. During a selection in similar circumstances on July 28, 1941, the Polish Franciscan missionary priest Maksymilian Rajmund Kolbe stepped forward and asked to be included in the group marked for death in the place of one of the despairing man who was chosen. After surviving for two weeks, Father Maksymilian Kolbe was put to death by phenol injection.

April 1941 – Prisoners began work on the construction of the Buna-Werke, walking 7 kilometers to the building site each morning and 7 kilometers back after work.

July 28, 1941 – a special commission arrives in Auschwitz and selects 575 prisoners, mostly Poles, to die in the euthanasia program for the "incurably ill"; the commission sends them to Sonnenstein, where they are put to death with carbon monoxide.

September 3, 1941 – approximately 600 Soviet POWs and 250 prisoners selected in the camp hospital were put to death with Zyklon B in the cellars of Block No. 11.

October 7, 1941 – the first mass transport of Soviet POWs arrived and was housed in 9 blocks fenced off to create the Russisches Kriegsgefangenenarbeitslager (Russian POW labor camp).

November 11, 1941 – the first execution at the "Death Wall" in the courtyard of Block No. 11. The condemned men were led singly to the wall, stripped naked and with their hands fettered behind their backs. The executions were performed by a point-blank shot to the nape of the neck with a small-caliber weapon.

Early 1942 – the beginning of the mass killing of Jews in the gas chambers.

March 1942 – the separate camp for Soviet POWs was liquidated. The approximately 900 POWs remaining alive, and some prisoners, were transferred to the camp in Brzezinka (Birkenau), which was still under construction.

March 26, 1942 – the first transports of women arrived: 999 prisoners from Ravensbrück and 999 Jewish women from Poprad, Slovakia. A separate women's division (Frauenabteilung), subordinated to the office of the commandant of Ravensbrück, was set up in Blocks No. 1–10.

April 1942 – the first provisional gas chamber in Birkenau, known as "Bunker No. 1" or "the little red house", was set up in a specially adapted farmhouse. The bodies of the victims were buried in mass graves in a nearby meadow.

June 10, 1942 – mutiny by prisoners in the penal company. Nine prisoners escaped, 13 were shot while attempting to escape, 20 more were shot during roll call, and about 320 were murdered in the gas chambers.

July 4, 1942 – the beginning of regular selections of Jews arriving in RSHA transports.

July 17–18, 1942 – Himmler's second visit (he watched the selection of an arriving transport of Jews, killing by gas in Bunker No. 2, and the "emptying of the bunker".

August 6, 1942 – start of the transfer of women prisoners from Auschwitz to Birkenau sector BIa.

September 1942 – the open-air burning of corpses exhumed from mass graves began in Birkenau; approximately 100,000 bodies burned in this way through the end of November.

October 28, 1942 – the largest execution in the history of the camp. After morning roll call, approximately 280 prisoners were taken under heavy SS guard to Block No. 11 and shot there in reprisal for sabotage and partisan operations in the Lublin region.

October 26, 1942 – approximately 500 prisoners from the Main Camp were chosen to be transferred to the newly opened sub-camp in the village of Monowice (from which civilians have been expelled), near where the IG Farbenindustrie factory is under construction. The sub-camp is named Buda and is a part of Auschwitz.

February 26, 1943 – arrival of the first transport of Gypsy families. They were placed in Birkenau sector BIIe, which was named the Zigeunerlager.

March 22, 1943 – the first of four crematorium buildings with gas chambers went into operation in Birkenau.

July 19, 1943 – 12 Polish prisoners from the surveyors' detail were hanged in reprisal for the escape of three prisoners from the detail. A collective gallows was built in the square in front of the kitchen. The execution was held in view of all the prisoners, after evening roll call.

September 8, 1943 – a transport of Jews arrived from the Theresienstadt ghetto-camp. They were placed in Birkenau sector BIIb, named the Famielienlager – Theresienstadt. The camp was liquidated in two stages in March and July 1944.

November 11, 1943 – Arthur Liebehenschel succeeded Rudolf Höss as commandant of Auschwitz.

November 22, 1943 – Auschwitz divided into three autonomous concentration camps: Auschwitz I – Stammlager (the Main Camp); Auschwitz II-Birkenau; and Auschwitz III-Aussenlager.

May 1944 – the extermination of the Hungarian Jews begins. More than 400 thousand Jews arrive through July, the majority of whom are murdered in the gas chambers.

August 2, 1944 – liquidation of the Gypsy family camp in Birkenau, *Zigeunerlager*.

August 12, 1944 – the first transport of civilians arrested on a mass scale after the start of the Warsaw Uprising arrived in Auschwitz II-Birkenau.

October 7, 1944 – mutiny by members of the *Sonderkommando*, resulting in the destruction of Crematorium IV.

January 17, 1945 – the final roll call in Auschwitz-Birkenau.

January 17–18, 1945 – the start of the evacuation march. After three days, the majority of approximately 60 thousand prisoners arrived on foot in Wodzisław Śląski and Gliwice, from where trains carried them to concentration camps in the depths of Germany.

January 27, 1945 – the liberation of Auschwitz by the Soviet army.

Glossary

Aufseherin – female SS overseer. These women were not members of the SS, but signed contracts with the commandant of a particular concentration camp. First appeared in Auschwitz in March 1942.

Blockführer – see **Principal functions held by SS men in the concentration camps.**

Camp Numbers – prisoners in German concentration camps were designated by numbers, which replaced their names. In Auschwitz, there were separate series of numbers for men, women, Soviet POWs, reeducation and police prisoners, and Roma. Until the spring of 1944, numbers from the main series (men and women) were assigned to Jews arriving in mass transports. Separate number series for Jews (separate series for men and women), beginning with the letters A and B, were introduced in May 1944. Only the few Jews arriving from other concentration camps continued to receive numbers from the main series. Auschwitz was the only camp where the numbers were tattooed on the prisoner's body. Tattoos were introduced because of the high death rate and difficulties with identifying large numbers of corpses. Tattoos were not applied to German prisoners, police and reeducation prisoners, Poles deported from Warsaw during the Uprising, and the majority of Jews deported after May 1944, who were placed in the so-called transit camps in Auschwitz II-Birkenau.

Functionaries (prisoner functionaries) – prisoners designated as direct supervisors of other prisoners in the camp and labor details. Prisoner functionaries included **Lagerälteste** (senior prisoner) had authority over all other overseers; **Blockälteste** (senior block prisoner, block supervisor) oversaw a building (block, barracks) where prisoners lived, responsible for order, food distribution, and counting the prisoners at roll call; **Schreiber** (scribe) assistant to the block supervisor, kept records on prisoners housed in a given building; **Stubendienst** (room supervisor) responsible for order in a room or part of a room; **Nachtwache** (night watchman) watched that no one went in or out of the building at night; **Arbeitsdienst** prisoner in charge of the work of a labor detail employed in an SS-man's office, director of the labor service (*Arbeitsdienstführer*), whose main task was administering the prisoner labor details; **Kapo** (capo) head of a labor detail, sometimes had assistants (**Unterkapo**) and **Vorarbeiters** (foremen, stewards), in charge of up to 20 prisoners. The largest labor details, numbering hundreds or even a thousand prisoners, were directed by an **Oberkapo**.

Geheime Staatspolizei, **Gestapo** – the secret political police in the Third Reich, founded in 1933. In 1939, shifted from the structure of the Ministry of Internal Affairs to the Main Reich Security Office. Its task was to combat political opposition and uphold the Nazi regime by means including the imprisonment of suspect persons in concentration camps. Gestapo functionaries worked in the Political Departments in these camps. Adolf Eichmann, responsible to a large degree for the extermination of the Jews during the war, headed Department IVB, the Jewish office in the Gestapo. In occupied countries, the Gestapo was the main instrument of terror and fought the resistance movement. The International Military Tribunal in Nuremberg declared the Gestapo to be a criminal organization responsible for crimes against humanity.

Kommando – a labor detail – a group of prisoners assigned to carry out specific labor under the supervision of an SS man functioning as *Kommandoführer* (group leader) and subordinate capos (one or several). These groups numbered from several to several hundred prisoners.

Lagerführer – see **Principal functions held by SS men in the concentration camps**, *Schutzhaftlagerführer*.

Lagerkommendant – see **Principal functions held by SS men in the concentration camps.**

Main Camp – the first and oldest part of the Auschwitz complex, founded in 1940. In the fall of 1940, the Nazis began building the second part of the camp in the nearby village of Brzezinka. The camp complex also included farms and industrial plants. In November 1943, the camp was divided into three parts: Auschwitz I – Stammlager (the Main Camp), Auschwitz II-Birkenau, and Auschwitz III-Monowitz (10 industrial sub-camps with a commandant's office in Monowice).

Principal functions held by SS men in the concentration camps:
    Blockführer – SS NCO overseeing the prisoners in a given block, and direct supervisor of all the prisoner functionaries in the block.
    Lagerkommendant – concentration camp commandant. In command of all the SS men in the camp garrison. Responsible for all aspects of the operation of the camp. From 1942, director of all the branches of SS companies operating on the grounds of the camp.
    Rapportführer – SS NCO. Duties included submitting reports on the number of prisoners as determined at the daily roll call.
    Schutzhaftlagerführer – concentration camp director. In charge of the prisoners in the camp. Reported directly to the camp commandant.

Righteous among the Nations of the World – a decoration in the form of a medal and a diploma on the basis of a special act of the parliament of Israel, the Knesset, in 1953. The award is granted to persons who are not citizens of Israel, and who risked their lives, out of humanitarian impulses to rescue Jews during the Second World War. It may also be awarded posthumously. The awards are granted with the approval of the Council for the Righteous among the Nations of the World at Yad Vashem (the Heroes' and Martyrs' Remembrance Authority) in Jerusalem. Trees in honor of the Righteous were formerly planted at the Institute; since the 1990s, when all the available space was filled, the names of the Righteous have been inscribed on stone tablets. As of 2006, 5,941 Poles constituted the most numerous group among the overall total of 21,310 Righteous.

Sonderkommando (German for "special working party"). A group made up of prisoners, mostly Jewish, used for removing corpses from the gas chambers, cutting hair, removing gold teeth, and burning the bodies in the crematoria. As direct eyewitnesses of the extermination of the Jews, the members of the *Sonderkommando* were strictly isolated. The prisoners laboring at Crematorium IV mutinied on October 7, 1944. In response, the SS killed more than 450 people. Three SS men died. The remaining members of the *Sonderkommando* were evacuated in January 1945, and several dozen of them survived until liberation.

SS man – lowest rank in the SS (see **SS ranks**). Former prisoners frequently use the term to refer to guards or escorts.

SS Ranks:

SS-Mann	– private
SS-Sturmann	– no equivalent
SS-Rottenführer	– private first class / lance corporal
SS-Unterscharführer	– corporal
SS-Oberscharführer	– sergerant
SS-Hauptscharführer	– first sergeant / master sergeant
SS-Sturmscharführer	– sergeant major
SS-Untersturmführer	– second lieutenant
SS-Obersturmführer	– first lieutenant
SS-Hauptsturmführer	– captain
SS-Sturmbannführer	– major
SS-Obersturmbannführer	– lieutenant colonel
SS-Standartenführer	– colonel
SS-Oberführer	– no equivalent
SS-Brigadeführer	– brigadier general

based on Rürup, ed., *Topography of Terror* (Berlin, 1989), p. 227.

Sub-camp – a branch camp (branch) of Auschwitz Concentration Camp. Beginning in 1942, sub-camps were opened near industrial facilities, mines, mills, and farms. Until November 1943, they were subordinated to the camp commandant in Auschwitz. When Auschwitz was divided into three camps, the industrial sub-branches fell under the commandant of Auschwitz III-Monowitz Concentration Camp, while the sub-camps at farms reported to the commandant of Auschwitz II-Birkenau. A *Lagerführer* (camp director), named by the commandant, was in charge of each sub-camp. More than 40 sub-camps of Auschwitz operated from 1942 to 1945, with up to several hundred prisoners laboring in each of them. The largest sub-camps, with more than a thousand prisoners laboring in each of them, included Blech-hammer, Eintrachthütte, Fürstengrube, Gleiwitz I, Günthergrube, Jawischowitz, and Monowitz (where more than 10 thousand prisoners labored).

Third Reich – popular term for the Nazi German state from 1933 to 1945.

Vistula-Oder Offensive – Soviet military operation lasting from January 12 to February 3, 1945. The Red Army began the offensive from staging areas along the right bank of the Vistula from the mouth of the Narew in the north to Jasło in the south, achieving the line of the Oder after 23 days of fighting in which they took Małopolska (including Krakow and Oświęcim), Upper Silesia, Mazovia, and Wielkopolska.

Wehrmacht – the armed forces of the Third Reich, created in March 1935 to replace the Reichswehr after the introduction by Adolf Hitler of conscription in contravention of the Versailles Treaty. The Wehrmacht included the army (Heer), air force (Luftwaffe), and navy (Kriegsmarine), directed by the Oberkommando der Wehrmacht (OKW). The first supreme commander of the armed forces was Field Marshal Werner von Blomberg, succeeded on January 27, 1938 by Adolf Hitler, who held the post until April 30, 1945. There were 4 million soldiers, airmen, and sailors in the Wehrmacht in 1939, and 11 million five years later. During the Second World War, 4.7 million Wehrmacht servicemen died on all fronts. After the war, the International Military Tribunal sat in judgment on the war crimes of the Wehrmacht.

Bibliography

If you found this subject interesting, you can find more information about the evacuation, liquidation, and liberation of the camp in the scholarly literature and memoirs. Here are some suggestions:

Apostoł-Staniszewska, Janina. *Nim zbudził się dzień*. Warsaw 1979.

Bellert, Józef. Praca polskich lekarzy i pielęgniarek w Szpitalu Obozowym PCK w Oświęcimiu po oswobodzeniu obozu, *Przegląd Lekarski*, 1:66–69, 1963.

Fiderkiewicz, Alfred, *Brzezinka. Wspomnienia z obozu*. Warsaw 1965.

Fudziński, Jerzy. *Marsz śmierci*. Jastrzębie Zdrój 1983.

Informator Towarzystwa Miłośników Miasta Żory 1993, No. 22 (articles on the passage of the evacuation march through Żory).

Jaworski, Czesław. *Wspomnienia z Oświęcimia*. Warsaw 1962.

Kielar, Wiesław. *Anus Mundi. Wspomnienia oświęcimskie*. Krakow 1976.

Kret, Józef. *Ostatni krąg*. Krakow 1973.

Numery mówią. *Wspomnienia więźniów KL Auschwitz*. Katowice 1980.

Pęckowski, Zbigniew. *Wspomnienia oświęcimskie*. Krakow 1977.

Piątkowska, Antonina. *Wspomnienia oświęcimskie*. Krakow 1977.

Strzelecki, Andrzej. *Evacuation, Dismantling and Liberation of KL Auschwitz*. Oświęcim 2001.

Strzelecki, Andrzej. *Ostatnie dni obozu Auschwitz*. Oświęcim 1995.

Strzelecki, Andrzej. *Marsz śmierci. Przewodnik po trasie do Wodzisławia Śląskiego*. Katowice 1989.

Szefer, Andrzej. *Miejsca straceń ludności cywilnej województwa katowickiego 1939–1945*. Katowice 1969.

Szachewicz, Mieczysław. *Noce bez świtu. Wspomnienia z Oświęcimia i Neuengamme*. Warsaw 1973.

Wspomnienia z niemieckich obozów koncentracyjnych, Ebensee 1946, Za pięć dwunasta, Warsaw 1973.

Żywulska, Krystyna. *I survived Auschwitz*. Warsaw 2004.

Contents